THE DALAI LAMA

ENDORSEMENT

Just as our own lives matter to us, the life of each individual creature is important to it. We share the same experience of pain and pleasure. As we assume the concerns of others, either in practice or in thought, compassion will flourish within us. In her new book, *The Lambs*, Carole George shares the fulfillment she has experienced over years tending a flock of sheep. If we lack affection for other creatures, our intellectual superiority becomes meaningless and can even be detrimental. I hope that this book will inspire readers to become more compassionate toward the living beings deprived of the many privileges we humans enjoy.

February 1, 2017

Praise for *The Lambs* by Carole George

"*The Lambs* is more than a charming story of an international lawyer who trades her professional practice for life with a flock of pet sheep. This is a thoughtful document that dispels any assumptions that sheep are 'just dumb farm animals' who do nothing but follow.

The author spent hours every day with her sheep, developing a deep word-less communication with them and sharing in their emotional lives—their mischief, the politics within the flock, and their expressions of grief. While never overly humanizing the sheep, she details the distinct personalities they develop in their unique situation of having her constant care and being part of outdoor meals and piano recitals in the barn.

Carole George is particularly convincing as she describes the subtlety with which the sheep formed personal relationships with her and her elderly father. She shows how the experience with them completely transformed her life, thereby making this book an impressive testament to the influence animals can exert on us and what they have to teach us.

Finally, science has admitted that we humans are not the only beings with personalities, emotions, and consciousness. *The Lambs* is an enchanting book. We all know young lambs frolic in the spring fields: now we learn about the fascinating social life of their elders. Please read this book."

—*Dr. Jane Goodall, DBE, founder of the Jane Goodall Institute and UN Messenger of Peace*

"This is a deeply spiritual book from an unexpected source, a former interna-tional lawyer who discovered the value of rootedness in a particular place, and through a quite unexpected influence, thirteen Karakul sheep. Whereas in their native Asian context the lambs are slaughtered in the millions for their pelts at a few days old, Carole George allowed them to grow naturally, with some of them reaching a full span of ten years, during which time a real friendship and mutual respect developed. Each day would begin with Carole and the sheep walking together round her small Virginia homestead, with the sheep's pace slowing down the author's, so that she came to appreciate the poetry of the landscape as never before. Indeed, like Little Sparta, the Scottish garden of the artist-poet Ian Hamilton Finlay, stones were soon being inscribed with significant, related lines of verse.

But it is the sheep who are throughout centre stage, with their individual characters fully described (whether playful, grumpy, affectionate or proud) and various stories told of their participating in tea-parties, concerts and sleeping arrangements: stories that never degenerate into the merely sentimental but rather acknowledge each of them as a unique gift that broadens the author's horizons. Not least does this happen in the encounter of each with death, which of necessity (given the number of health problems to which they are subject) is a theme that runs throughout the book. Their individual life-stories are intertwined with a moving account of an elderly father also approaching death. The result is a real sense of what it is to reverence the lives of all creatures, an awareness of what it means to let go, and yet at the same time carry in one's memories values that transfigure not only the departed but also those who remain.

A beautifully written book whose poetic, evocative style can be confidently recommended to all who are seeking something different out of where and how they live, and the animals with whom they seek to relate."

—*David Brown, FBA, author of* God and Enchantment of Place

"When Carole George found sheep, the sheep found her, and, in writing about what she learned, she helps modern readers find themselves. We live in isolated, digital bubbles, and her vision of finding one's home, being on a quest there, and discovering meaning in daily experience, is all the evidence we need to pass the right verdict on the excesses of our civilization and recover our lost values.

The sheep taught her how to communicate with other orders of creation, to see music in life, and to discover how the distant past in Samarkand meets 21st-century Virginia. Her lambs taught her that she had a gift to write, and her readers will delight in the way she uses this gift to illuminate the meaning and purpose of the human journey."

—*Father Laurence Freeman, OSB, World of Community for Christian Meditation*

"*The Lambs* is the unusual story of a small flock of sheep, originally bred for meat, who are allowed to live out long natural lives on a farm in Virginia. They grow from young lambs into mature individuals with distinct characters, showing how thoughtful care affects animals. Carole George skillfully demonstrates the depth of the relationship that can develop between farm animals and their caretaker. Not only do the sheep thrive, their gentle company completely transforms the author's life."

 —*Gene Baur, Chief Executive, Farm Sanctuary*

"*The Lambs* is beautifully written, and right on target as an example of the natural—in this case pastoral—world where we may achieve the fullness of human experience. When, in the 22nd century perhaps, we've settled down as a species and reached sustainability and much fuller self-knowledge, our descendants may have gravitated toward the equivalent of Carole George's Virginia farm."

 —*Edward O. Wilson, University Research Professor Emeritus, Harvard University*

"We grant cats and dogs personalities and emotional lives, and do the same for charismatic animals such as apes and elephants, while conveniently leaving farm animals out of the picture. But there is no good reason why they should be any different. After reading Carole George's warm and charming account of her life with a small flock of Karakuls, you will never again look at sheep as an undifferentiated mass."

 —*Frans de Waal, Ph.D., author of* Are We Smart Enough to Know How Smart Animals Are?

"In this deeply moving, true-life story, Carole George highlights how the humility and calmness of her sheep brought peace and fulfillment into her active professional life. She demonstrates that respect for individuals of other species can open our eyes to forgotten values and sweep away the arrogance of *speciesism*."

 —*Richard D. Ryder, author of* Victims of Science, Animal Revolution, The Political Animal, *and* Speciesism, Painism and Happiness

"Nearly all Americans can relate to stories of immigration, and they know how immigrants can enrich our world. However, Carole George's immigrants are absolutely unique in that they are not human beings but Karakul sheep descended from Central Asia. Assigning them names like Chopin and Debussy, George appreciatively studies their lives and highly distinctive personalities at her farm in Virginia. By the end of this charming book we feel we know these black, beige, and reddish heirs of the world of Tamerlane and Chengiz Khan."

—*S. Frederick Starr, Central Asia Institute, Johns Hopkins University*

"Carole George's beautiful and poignant book is as much about her scholarly, poetry-loving father as it is about her endearing pet sheep. In ten years' time she learns the strengths and weaknesses of the breed she has chosen, develops a close relationship with some individuals in particular, and learns to lead a quiet life as the keeper of her flock, in tune with the rhythms of nature. In elegant, musical cadences she presents a quiet meditation on the beauty all around us and the fleeting but precious opportunity to share our lives with other souls. Scenes of her playing the piano surrounded by a captivated audience of sheep and her father's touching relationship with his favorite sheep, Satie, are unforgettable."

—*Bob Tarte, author of* Enslaved by Ducks, Fowl Weather, Kitty Cornered, *and* Feather Brained

"If you ever wanted to know what it is like to be a lamb, please read this book. Smart, emotional, inquisitive, curious, playful, and loving, these wonderful beings, and Carole George's stories about her life with them, will at once educate, inspire, and surprise you. We are living in an epoch called The Anthropocence, often called 'the age of humanity.' I like to call it 'the rage of inhumanity.' It is essential that we evolve as fast as possible toward more peaceful and less violent ways of interacting with our animal kin in an increasingly human-dominated world. The time has come—indeed, it is long overdue—to use what we *know about the fascinating and diverse inner lives of other animals on their behalf. The Lambs* will surely move people to do something for the billions of nonhumans who need all the help they can get."

—*Marc Bekoff, Professor Emeritus of Ecology and Evolutionary Biology at the University of Colorado, Boulder, and author of* Rewilding Our Hearts: Building Pathways of Compassion and Coexistence *and* The Animals' Agenda: Freedom, Compassion, and Coexistence in the Human Age

"This enchanting parable is about the continuum of being. Our Shepherdess and her Karakul flock from Bokhara develop relationships which are near to human.

Elegiacally set in the shadow of the Blue Ridge Mountains of Virginia, the life and death of her thirteen sheep elide ideas from Sufism, Darwinism, Lorenz and elsewhere, Kant for example. That our witness has been an international U.S. attorney is remarkable. More important, it makes her critique of our present priorities, and let us not mince words, appetites, more telling and timely. It is a tale that should be available in both primary schools and Business Class lounges. Simple, poetic, and tender, it seeks to move the soul of man in his stewardship of creation."

—*Michael Brophy, chief executive of Charities Aid Foundation (1982–2002)*

The Lambs

The Lambs

My Father, a Farm,
and the Gift of a Flock of Sheep

Carole George

THOMAS DUNNE BOOKS
St. Martin's Press
New York

THOMAS DUNNE BOOKS.

An imprint of St. Martin's Press.

THE LAMBS. Copyright © 2018 by Carole Shelbourn George, LLC.
Printed in China. For information, address
St. Martin's Press, 175 Fifth Avenue, New York, N.Y. 10010.

www.thomasdunnebooks.com

www.stmartins.com

Designed by Kathryn Parise

LIBRARY OF CONGRESS CATALOGING-IN-PUBLICATION DATA

Names: George, Carole Shelbourn, author.
Title: The lambs : my father, a farm, and the gift of a flock of sheep / Carole George.
Description: New York : Thomas Dunne Books, an imprint of St. Martin's Press, 2018. |
Includes bibliographical references.
Identifiers: LCCN 2017051030 | ISBN 9781250113528 (hardcover) | ISBN 9781250113535 (ebook)
Subjects: LCSH: George, Carole Shelbourn. | Lawyers—United States—Biography.
Classification: LCC KF373.G463 A3 2018 | DDC 630.92 [B]—dc23
LC record available at https://lccn.loc.gov/2017051030

Our books may be purchased in bulk for promotional, educational, or business use.
Please contact your local bookseller or the
Macmillan Corporate and Premium Sales Department at
1-800-221-7945, extension 5442, or by email
at MacmillanSpecialMarkets@macmillan.com.

First Edition: April 2018

10 9 8 7 6 5 4 3 2 1

To Mary Midgley,

in friendship and admiration

Contents

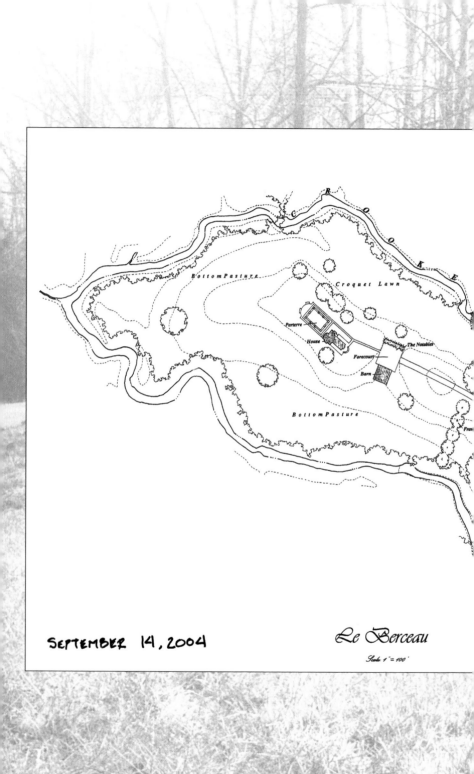

C R O O K E

Bottom Pasture

Croquet Lawn

Parterre

House

Forecourt

The Notables

Barn

Bottom Pasture

SEPTEMBER 14, 2004

Le Berceau

Scale 1" = 100'

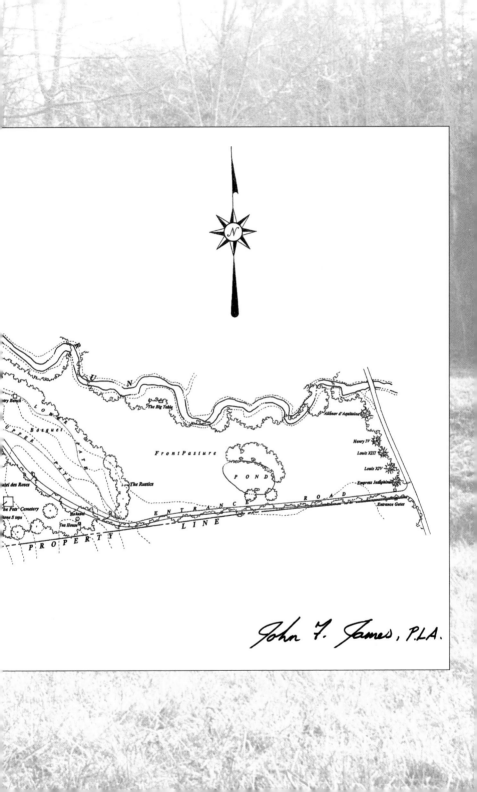

John F. James, P.L.A.

Part One

 ## INITIATION

Responding to the Call

1

Landscape of the Mind

A country setting, a wide expanse of pasture. The grass is green but no longer has that rich hue of early summer. A shallow pond is in the center of the field. A stream runs along the far side; old maples and sycamores line its bank. On the other side is a wooded area that is thick with leaning trees and piles of rotten logs. It appears to continue in deepening shades of green all the way to the black silhouette of distant mountains.

Beside the pond is a rickety green bench. An elderly man sits at one end, reading from the book that lies open on his lap. White hair sneaks out from under his rumpled wool hat. He wears ironed blue jeans, a tweed jacket frayed at the cuffs, red socks, sturdy shoes. At the other end of the bench is a much younger woman. She has brown chin-length hair and is wearing a long sweater over a wool skirt. Her gaze falls on the man, who is reading to her.

You cannot miss the family resemblance: high cheekbones,

carved jaws, almost identical profiles, two sets of penetrating light blue eyes, intelligent but at the same time tender. They both hold their heads with a sense of assurance. The atmosphere enveloping them is as tranquil as the scene all around.

This morning, I am sitting with my eighty-five-year-old father, who could not wait to visit the little farm in central Virginia I acquired two months ago. His forebears, planters from England, settled in Colonial Virginia, near Richmond. He has often mentioned how much he would have liked to attend the University of Virginia, I suppose to reconnect to those early family roots. Now, to have a claim to a scrap of Virginia countryside is irresistible. That the place is a shambles doesn't matter.

For decades, he and I have read to each other. Even on business trips, this is how we would pass the time on long flights. We have worked our way through various translations of the *Odyssey* and the *Iliad*, Plato, Aristotle, all of Shakespeare, and his cherished English Romantic poets. For this visit, we select the *Aeneid* and are proceeding through King Evander's reflections on the glorious reign of his predecessor, Saturn. At a stopping place, my father carefully marks the page with a strip of old leather. He closes the book slowly. His hands, although capable of performing any task, are stiffer than they were even a year ago. I assume I will be hearing an observation about the Golden Age.

He turns to me and says, "Honey, you know what this farm needs?"

I brace myself. A lot of money? At least a tractor?

He says, "This is 'poetry country.' This ground calls for sheep."

2

Consecration

"Poetry country." It is not the first time I have heard my father describe a landscape in this way. His mind, shaped by years of reading Greek and Latin classic verse and decades of memorizing the works of his beloved William Wordsworth, seeks out such places.

But this morning, his poetic vision is so intense that I, too, can see it as we gaze down a long grassy expanse inside the belt of shade trees along the edge of the stream. If Theocritus could manufacture his pastoral inventions of eternal spring out of bare, rocky Arcady, we ought to be able to find a pastoral setting underneath a thicket of scrub trees. But that is only half of it.

"This ground calls for sheep." Did he say *Sheep*? This part is new. I've never heard him say this about any scene. Perhaps he is thinking of what Virgil did with his inventory of stage properties, which invariably included a stream, a shade tree, mild breezes, a flower-strewn meadow, and a small flock of sheep.

Front pasture. On that first day, my father and I sat on this old bench, which has never been moved from its original position beside the murky little pond. In the intervening years, the bench has received numerous coats of dark green paint, the fields have been cleaned and clarified, and The Lambs have laid out a network of paths in the forest. If you look very carefully, you will see a hint of the Big Table on the far right.

But I will always believe that there was something deeper contained in those words. They carry all the seriousness of a consecration. They remind me of something I've read, that the Greek equivalent for the word *consecration* connotes newness and renewal. Whatever prompted his declaration that the ratty little farm is a poetic landscape requiring sheep makes no difference. What matters is that it has claimed his heart. The father who chanted, "International, international, everything is going to be international" during my school years has reversed the trajectory. Forget the international. Now is a time to dwell. To attune myself to the stillness of the place. As Saint Augustine said, "Seek not to venture forth: turn within. Truth dwelleth in the inner man."

I already know that in arriving here I have crossed a threshold. Today it is set aside as a sacred precinct. His book and the leather bookmark and the old bench, all of these are now precious icons that will accompany us through our years here, reminding us of the existence of an immaterial world beyond our own. And sheep? Yes, there will be sheep.

3

"Weekend Retreat"

Just why I had been glancing through the rural property ads in
The Washington Post at seven o'clock that Sunday morning, I will
probably never know. Here is what I read: "Weekend retreat. 27
acres, north of Orange, Virginia. Grand piano conveys with the
property." The minute I saw the word *piano*, I knew the place was
meant for me. My piano is my most treasured possession and the
source of the music I carry around in my head all the time.

The drive from Washington had taken less than an hour and a
half. The half-mile gravel lane leading into the property was like a
tunnel of leaves. Hickories and tulip-poplars, oaks and maples met
overhead as in an arbor.

It was easy to see that the place had not been maintained. The
elderly owners wanted to return to their families in Massachusetts.
They were selling the farm themselves. It was affordable. There was
no negotiation.

The house was modest but situated to take in the distant Blue Ridge Mountains. Crooked Run, the boundary line, reminded me of the river that cut through my grandfather's ground and of the sweet little trickle of water that ran behind the upstate New York home of my first boyfriend.

The lid of the old piano was blistered and peeling. It had chipped ivory keys that looked like a bad set of teeth, but it could be played, and it wasn't even terribly out of tune. I will always believe that this farm was waiting for me. That I was lifted out of my world by invisible hands and deposited here. And while I hastened to claim it as my own little realm, I have never had the slightest sense of proprietary possession. It is far too precious to have a price.

The former owners left behind some basic battered furniture. Though I was certainly not set up to receive an important guest, my father wanted to visit. I didn't remember inviting him, and I was a little concerned about what he would think of this hovel. Too late. He was on his way.

He would stay in a downstairs room, from which he could see one long expanse of pasture. We took slow walks around the perimeter, admiring the stream and reminiscing about the farm of his youth. One night, I saw an odd light moving around in the lower pasture. I waited until my eyes adjusted to the darkness. He was out there with a flashlight.

We spent a day in Charlottesville, and on the way back to the farm, we stopped at the Orange-Madison Farmers' Cooperative, which I proudly joined. We purchased a couple of rakes and a broom, and he gathered a supply of leather gloves.

This was a Saturday. The next morning, we took our copies of the *Aeneid* down to the bench beside the murky pond. And the little farm took on its new identity as "poetry country."

4

In Search of Sheep

My father leans on his walking stick to rise from the bench. I can't help noticing that as we make our way back to the house, his pace has quickened slightly. We have a purpose. We spread peanut butter on saltines and pour a glass of red wine, and we are ready to set out to find the only area sheep breeder who answers his telephone on a Sunday morning.

What are we thinking? I have one friend who never stops insisting that I—of the legendary organized mind—had to have been planning for animals all along. But I know I was not. This was entirely my father's idea, and I quite simply accepted the notion of sheep as a sign of grace. That's all I can say.

Newborn lambs? I've never known one, never looked into one's eyes. I've never even touched one. I'm so excited, I can barely speak.

My father carefully arranges his legs in the passenger's seat of my old Mercedes, and off we go. This is not the first time he and I have set forth. There were road trips across America in my early years. I will never forget the first one. He was delivering a little red sports car before I started my first job at the National Endowment for the Arts in Washington, D.C. Through the Iowa cornfields and the hog farms of Ohio, he entertained me with stories of his youth in Missouri. This was the first time (but not the last) that I heard about his expeditions into caves deep in the hills near that gracious old farm. Can you imagine a ten-year-old boy crawling to the back of a network of caves to spend the night? His poor mother.

His father would give him tasks, such as moving a herd of cattle from one pasture to another. This was when he was eleven or twelve years old. He told me these tales with a degree of pride. "You know, honey, I realized later that Father did not need to have those cattle moved. He gave me these assignments so I would develop the confidence that I could carry out his wishes. Oh, and I remember one time Father asked me to take a dozen full-grown cattle into town to sell. Even back then it wasn't common to see a young boy doing such a thing, and a couple people told him they had stopped what they were doing to watch me."

5

The Source of Sheep

We turn off one gravel road after another until we work our way up to the most far-flung margins of Washington. Twenty-five miles from Dulles International Airport, the route is lined with large dairy farms interspersed with shanties, so typical of the American South. The breeder's road skirts a small pasture and ends under a carport attached to a conventional suburban house.

I am always asked why my sheep are Karakuls. Simple. On this Sunday morning, only one breeder listed in the local directory answered the telephone. I have no knowledge of the different breeds of sheep. As far as I know, sheep are all of the same breed, always white and immobile, heads bent down to eat grass or bodies reclining on the ground. Soon the exotic Karakul heritage will capture my imagination, but today, remember, I am furnishing a poetic landscape. The breed of the sheep is irrelevant.

My father introduces us. The breeder is unimpressed. No handshake is on offer. On the telephone, I made the mistake of telling him I wanted lambs for pets. "Pets!"

I could almost see him rolling his eyes. (Pets, and now a handshake? You gotta be kidding!) Most customers purchase lambs for breeding stock. Others are contacted when meat is available. The long coarse Karakul wool, famous for carpets and felt making, is highly prized in the fiber arts.

My purpose is so dubious, he does not waste his time on the history of his animals. He spits out that they are of a rare breed from Central Asia and that they are considered fur-bearing sheep because they produce what we know as Persian Lamb. That's it. He shoves a one-page fact sheet into my hand and whirls around to lead us into his six-acre operation, a compact maze of temporary pens connected to an old wooden structure.

The bright September sun is swallowed in the low entrance room. I stoop to enter. Bales of hay and straw are crammed against the rough walls. The dirt floor is dusted with loose straw. Interior light filters through knotholes. Any other illumination comes from pairs of wary yellow eyes. One sleek gray barn cat glares: *No, lady, don't even think about petting my head.*

6

Three Ewe Lambs

Beyond this passage is a pen for mothers with their newborn ewe lambs. The air is thick with the musky scent of colostrum. I'm helplessly in love. Everyone and everything around me dissolves. I have no idea what my father is doing. I am here solely with these lambs, bewitched. I rush up to an infant lamb who stands between her mother's outstretched legs. There is no way to resist her, off-white like her mother, with tangerine curls parting across her nose. Loose white curls cover her little body. She has white eyelashes over downcast eyes. Her ears are long and narrow. She seems shy, but her mouth curves up in a girlish smile. She can't weigh more than eight or nine pounds.

I bend over to lift her onto my left shoulder, as I have often carried around a cat. I would be wary of a kitten's sharp claws, but here I have no concern in the world. This is the first member of my flock. I name her Debussy.

I have often thought of Debussy as my blood type. As a child, I would listen to my grandmother playing his music on the black grand piano that had been carried on a flatboat up the Mississippi River and carted across ground to the northern edge of Montana. I see so clearly that vast room, where several layers of bearskin rugs cover the floor. My old memory includes my grandfather's mellow baritone voice. After a day of supervising work on his vast grain ranch, he leans over my grandmother's shoulder as they explore pages of Debussy's songs that they purchased on their last trip to Paris.

When I was six, Shadow, my black spaniel puppy, died, and my mother chose piano lessons as the appropriate distraction. I had already found the piano music of Claude Debussy in a stack of family LPs. By the time I was ready for piano recitals, I had listened to Philippe Entremont's recording of the solo piano music so often that I had memorized "Clair de Lune" before seeing the sheet music.

Debussy lifted me out of my grandfather's barnyard into a sophisticated world of exquisitely polished cluster chords. I lived inside the preludes and arabesques, and when I was ready to compete in music competitions, I won every available award for my imitation of Entremont's rendering of "Clair de Lune." I veered off to study literature in college, but my love of the piano and the music of Claude Debussy will always be part of my life.

The lamb immediately behind Debussy is completely covered in shiny, tight ivory curls. Her thin face is sculpted into delicate features. She possesses none of Debussy's modesty. Her beady chestnut eyes stare straight at me, daring me to do something as silly as lift her onto my shoulder. Or touch her, for that matter. She is already, at three days old, fully aware of her distinct attributes. An important influence on the music of Debussy, she will be Mozart.

Then comes solid black Chopin. She has no curls on the top of her head; long, straight wool separates in the center to make it look flat. She is thick and wide across the back, and her bowed legs are shorter than those of my other two lambs. She stumps around in a narrow range beside her mother.

These are my ewes.

7

Ten Ram Lambs

The ram lambs and their mothers are in a long aisle on the other side of the hay-storage area. Daylight streams through unfinished window frames. Whatever happened to solid white sheep? Here is a gallery of polished jet black curls, purplish black, gleaming bronze, dark rust, and as many variations of white as bodies: ivory, ivory and bright white, ivory with beige markings, brown threaded through off-white, mottled gray and white, ivory with red streaks, ivory with red blotches.

My eyes light on the nearest curly beige one. He gazes confidently down his snout, summarizing his natural steady self-assurance. He will be my fourth lamb, Bach. He was born just a few hours ago, but he is already on his feet, standing taller than the others. While the other little males are peeping their medium-pitched chirps, Bach observes silently.

On the telephone, the breeder had told me that four is the mini-

mum number he will sell for a small flock. A ram and three healthy
ewes ought to be enough. But just beyond Bach is an amazing creature, entirely covered in shiny metallic copper curls like a great ball
of Brillo. "Can't I please have that one?" I beg.

Grumble. "Oh, I guess so." But the red one is the firstborn of
twins. Therefore, his pure black brother will have to come, too.
Three ewes and three rams.

Then a miracle occurs. A tiny black lamb tentatively approaches
me. I stand perfectly still. His little head is within inches of my right
shin. Now he rubs it against my ankle.

Three ewes and four rams.

⌒

A few weeks later, I decide to adopt a few more lambs. To the
breeder, I am just a silly woman who thinks of sheep as pets, and
I'm not surprised that he readily sells me six lambs who have been
sired by a ram who was there only temporarily. I don't care what
this man thinks of me. If I am a convenient disposal for a few woe-
fully small lambs, then I will happily slosh across a muddy field to
select them. Thirteen. Surely this is enough for someone whose animal experience is limited to two cats at any one time.

Couperin. (ABOVE RIGHT) *Several weeks after I had selected the seven older
lambs, I went back to the breeder for six more ram lambs. Here you see Couperin just a few days after he was born. I always suspected that the breeder
regretted letting me have Couperin because of the white poll on the top of his
head, a distinguishing feature of the Karakul sheep.*
Poulenc newly born. (BELOW RIGHT) *Baby Poulenc, born just hours before this
picture was taken, teeters beside his mother.*

Newborn Satie. Here I am with days-old Satie. His long tail will soon be docked. In time, the tails of Karakuls fill with fat and broaden to cover the entire backside of the sheep. If allowed to remain long, the tails grow too heavy to be carried comfortably.

8

Wethers

The lambs have two important preparations ahead of them. The breeder will immediately dock their tails. This is considered necessary for general hygiene and is supposedly not overly stressful to very young lambs. A heavy rubber band, called an elastrator, is placed around the tail at the desired length. It cuts off the blood supply, and as it gradually tightens, the unwanted portion of the tail dries and drops off.

The fat tail is a distinguishing Karakul feature. Richard Lydekker, in *The Sheep and Its Cousins*, describes it as two great cushions divided by a median cleft. Even shortened, the flat Karakul tail covers the entire rump and can weigh as much as thirty pounds. It is valued as "the butter of Central Asia." Some docked tails are very neat and tidily tucked in, as is Mozart's. More typically, the lower edge turns up in loose curls to form an S shape. At this young age, The Lambs' tails do not seem so different from those of other breeds. But over time, they fill with fat, so that it looks like they have pillows swaying on their backsides.

Next, the breeder asks if I want my male lambs to be castrated. If so, it is less painful if he does it now. He adds that if I decide to breed my ewes, I can always "rent a ram" or take them to another farm to be bred.

I suspect he knows that I will not be breeding sheep. The idea of pregnant ewes giving birth in tents in the middle of winter is just too much. But I have to ask whether castrating them will change their personalities. He assures me that, as wethers, they will have all the vigor of unaltered males. They will not develop full sets of Karakul horns, but neither will they break out of fences or crash through doors. I am persuaded, but I will not attend the surgery the next day.

I do not immediately make the connection between a castrated male lamb and the term *bellwether*. From ninth-century Old English, a bellwether is the one who demonstrates leadership abilities and is designated to wear the bell. I have visions of hanging brass bells of varying pitches on all my lambs, but this is not a good idea, warns the breeder. Karakul wool easily mats (hence its historic attractiveness to felt makers), and a ribbon around the neck causes the wool underneath to bond and trap moisture as a nursery for subcutaneous insect larvae.

If that is not sufficiently distasteful, the full connation of *bellwether* is. The bellwether is assigned the task of delivering the flock into the slaughterhouse. Next to the door is a hinged section of fencing, "the bellwether gate." The bellwether leads his trusting con-freres down the sheep run toward the open door of the slaughter-house. At the last moment, the shepherd pulls him through this gate as the others proceed to their unhappy destination. He is then placed among another flock to repeat the cycle.

9

Shepherdess

Had I thought to inquire, I would have been told that eight years is a normal long life for a Karakul sheep. But I am so overjoyed with my new creatures that I am not thinking about how long they will live or what illnesses might afflict them. Today, I operate inside a miracle, and realities, such as what I am to do when my numbers dwindle to three or two or (God forbid) one, do not enter my mind.

The breeder volunteers that sheep hide sickness as long as possible. If one refuses to eat or is unable to stand, he is probably beyond saving. A sheep found lying on the ground and straining his neck over one shoulder is dying. But this is simply too much for me to comprehend today.

"Well, look, I've gotta get on with my evening feeding," he says as he ambles off. I want to stay all night with my new lambs, but after another twenty minutes, I take his hint and go to say good-bye.

He is in a back pasture, walking down a slope behind a group of sheep. They are newly shorn ewes, perhaps ones who have not given birth this season. It is an unforgettable sight: a dozen variously colored sheep shambling along in front of the man, as unconcernedly as he apparently follows, with his blue denim shirt hanging down over his sloppy blue jeans.

That image (with the exception of the attire) becomes my goal. What I want more than anything else in the world is to stroll with such obvious ease down a little hillside behind my own flock.

Later that evening, I go back over the long day at the breeder's farm. It was certainly not an encounter with a basket of kittens or puppies tumbling over one another. Sheep may be highly social animals, but they do not interact with one another at this age. Remote and self-contained, each lamb stays with his mother as he quietly surveys his environment.

The gaze of a lamb has a force. It has already affected me. Is he simply observing me? Does he have some expectation of me? And what does he reveal of himself in that unremitting regard? The poet asks, "Little lamb, who made thee?" My question is basic: Who are you, little lamb?

I know the thrill of learning a new language and adjusting to changes in food, climate, and the manners of living in a foreign country. But now I have entered a world where there are no guidebooks or dictionaries, and where words are insignificant noises made with the mouth. I ask myself, Do I have the necessary sensitivity to communicate with my new lambs?

At this point, I remember a dream I have experienced a number of times in the past. In it, I am always alone in a dark theater, sitting in the center of the first row of seats.

There is a simple proscenium arch and a deep stage. There is no decoration. In the rear corner of stage left is a thick illuminated column emitting brilliant white light. It appears from above the stage and disappears below it.

The column is a shimmering spiral of fully grown white sheep, walking steadfastly in a line, around and around, looking straight ahead, continuously moving at a deliberate pace. The light is intense.

There is another version of the dream, identical except that the spiral of sheep progresses upward, arising mysteriously from below the stage and proceeding up and out of sight. The elusive mechanism continues until I wake up.

It has been a long time since I experienced either version of the dream, but I wonder, if I had that dream tonight, what would I make of that spiral of sheep, slowly circling down to my level and then continuing until they are out of my sight, below the stage. Today it occurs to me that it is left up to me to break their continuum: It is for me to invite them into my life.

But they are already in my life! They are occupying my interior world, there for some purpose. If, as many ancient traditions hold, animals in dreams are messengers, then today a message has been delivered. Out of my inner world and into my daily life, the lambs are carriers of my most valuable inheritance, the sound of my father's voice repeating the words and images of his dearly loved poetry.

10

Preparation

My father makes a few practical suggestions before he must return to my mother in Montana. The years have not been kind to my lovely mother, and by this time she is neither physically nor mentally able to travel.

He inspects the little white horse barn below the house. "They can live there very nicely for a while," he says. "They will need more room later on, but this is a good place for young lambs." A neighbor volunteers to fence several pastures connected to the shed. In the neighborhood, there is a lot of excitement about the new lambs; it will be easy to find whatever help I need.

The lambs will have to stay with their mothers for five or six months. During this time, I visit them far more often than the breeder appreciates. But he tolerates my presence by insisting I acquire certain basic sheep-management skills.

Halter training comes first. I may believe I am physically fit, but

I am not prepared for an afternoon of dragging live animals across a field. A lamb may submit to having a nylon halter slipped over his nose, but there his patience may end. Some simply lie down on the ground.

The swashbuckling copper male, whom I have named Ginastera, literally tangoes to the end of the pasture and back, gyrating around to show off his red curls. His body is always in motion, his lust for life equal to his blazing color. His solid black twin, the beguiling Saint-Saëns, is a surprisingly good student. Debussy requires a lot of encouragement to get going, but she makes an acceptable effort, as does Chopin. Of course the gallant Bach welcomes the invitation for high-step marching. He straightens his neck, fixes his eyes on the goal, and proceeds.

But I make the mistake of leaving Mozart to the last. She immediately flops down on her side. The breeder gives her one stiff shove to put her on her feet. This lasts for a few seconds. Then he stands back with his arms folded across his chest. I can hear him saying to himself, Okay, little lady, let's see what you can do with your pets, as Mozart collapses again. A glance at his smirk toughens my resolve. Under no circumstance will I throw the halter lead on the ground and run. If Mozart's performance takes the rest of the day, we will, well . . .

And I steer her one-hundred-pound body with my right hand while with my left hand I scoop her considerable bottom off the ground again and again, and again.

Very young lambs while still with breeder. Four of the older lambs are no longer solely in the company of their mothers. The white ewe lamb, Debussy, on the far right, stands beside Mozart. In the foreground are two of the pure black ram lambs, Fauré on the left and Saint-Saëns to his right. They are almost four months old in this picture.

11

Changes

Although it is late in the year, it is warm enough to sit on the old bench at the pond and watch large varnished leaves break off the sycamores and collide in the intense blue fall air. There is not the slightest hint of the melancholy that sometimes announces the coming of winter. Rather, there is a feeling of fullness in this autumn air. I realize this is how I feel—enlarged—that an entire world is opening up to me. I also know that I am facing a major decision, probably as significant as the one years ago that I did not aspire to both a career and motherhood.

I certainly know how much I've put into building my law practice. But here, in front of me, is an almost unfathomable opportunity to create a home for other creatures. Soon I shall be a shepherdess, known throughout antiquity as the representation of love and care, the guardian of the sanctuary of homecoming. This is not a matter of a cat or two in a city apartment. An entire flock of living beings is about to arrive.

When I started my small law firm, we were the only specialists exclusively devoted to counseling clients on the transfer of large charitable gifts from one country to another. Now there are attorneys in New York and London who practice in this area, and I have no doubt that I can responsibly figure out a strategy to place our ten faithful individual and international corporate clients in other capable hands.

The first test of my shepherdess skills will be within my own office. Fortunately, my four talented colleagues have visited the farm from the beginning, and they know exactly what's coming. I suppose I'm comforted that occasionally they've hinted about their desires to pursue fields other than our specialization.

One afternoon, my tax expert is strolling around the pasture with me. I ask him if he's really serious about exploring an in-house corporation position. He is, and we agree that the time has come to watch for good opportunities for him. When a friend tells me his law firm is going to be looking for a corporate tax attorney, a very successful transition is easily made. My most creative lawyer has just finished designing an education program for the Embassy of Japan. More than once, she has confessed that she wishes she had followed a career in art education rather than law. Here again, we get lucky, and by the end of the next year, she is the director of education at a major museum. Another loyal attorney is thrilled by my news because she has been longing to marry her boyfriend in England but has not wanted to abandon us.

By the time we have had these discussions, and it appears that everything is in order to go our separate ways, I am left with a sense that my move to the farm was somehow inevitable, part of a divine plan for my life. There is nothing holding me back. There are only doors opening on all sides.

12

Weaning

Before long, there is frost on car windows, and I can think of nothing except the normal 103-degree temperature of my thirteen woolly bodies. The breeder declares that I cannot visit them during Christmas week because he is expecting company. "Really?" I lament. "But didn't you tell me you can never find the strawberry wine you love? I wanted to give you what we found in New York." 'Tis the season to kill with kindness. And three bottles of strawberry liqueur buy almost daily visits to my lambs.

Back in Washington, a Christmas party ebbs away, leaving stacks of books and CDs under the tree. Several colleagues have brought me serious manuals on sheep raising. Lawyers are so parochial. Why would I want to read about sheep when I can spend my entire time with them? The young woman who sells me my business uniform of neat black suits cannot stop giggling when she presents a pair of Chanel leather clogs. My accountant, who grew up on a farm in Germany, says, "You may think they're ugly, but you keep them. You're going to need them."

Although witnessing the castration of my male lambs was out of the question, I am intrigued by the process of weaning. The mothers could accomplish this naturally because they have to regain their strength for future lambs; after a normal five- to six-month period of nursing, they simply begin to shun their lambs.

My breeder forces the separation. On the appointed day, early in the new year, he secures the lambs in one pen. They cannot see their mothers, who are confined together nearby. I arrive late in the afternoon. I haven't missed anything, he assures me. Nothing will happen until the end of the evening. As the sun fades, the lambs become restless, anxiously searching for their mothers. The mothers occasionally look up from their grazing, as though they have suddenly noticed that the lambs who have been standing beside them for months are missing.

Then the calling begins. At first, I hear a prolonged lowing. It gradually amplifies into a sustained cry. I will never forget the blanket of primitive anguish that reached across the farm in the early darkness. For the next twenty-four hours, the lambs will crowd into the corner of their pen closest to the sound of their mothers' voices and cry for them. The mothers, more relaxed about the process, intersperse their calling with walking around and cropping grass.

"Well, I guess we can deliver them anytime you want," the breeder announces. But in fact, we negotiate a boarding fee, and the weeks drag by as I continue to arrange the details of closing my firm. All I think about is my weekends with the lambs.

13

Origins

My weekends at the farm begin to stretch to include Fridays and sometimes even Mondays. Other than my visits to the lambs, I spend my time walking around the property. I catch myself strolling along the edge of the stream with a smile on my face. The pastures are littered with scrub trees, but gradually I begin to picture how they would look with all of these cleared away. I also take out a few books about my favorite French traditional gardens.

It would be wholly unsuitable—and certainly unaffordable—to attempt a French classic garden in the backwoods of Virginia. But I love the elegant simplicity of those old gardens and begin to imagine a few straight rows of trees and perhaps a garden beyond the house that is no more than a rectangle of sand paths.

When I go to visit the lambs, if the breeder is feeling generous, he might hand me a copy of an article about Karakul sheep. Today, he produces a 1919 *National Geographic* feature entitled "The Land of Lambskins," which describes the origin of these exotic sheep. The author states, "All camel trails in the Emirate of Bokhara, like the roads to Rome, lead to the marketplace in Bokhara City." There is an image of the Karakul bazaar, where piles of lambskins line one wall in stacks as tall as the men standing beside them.

One afternoon, he gives me a copy of an industry pamphlet that refers to the Karakuls' arrival in America in 1909. This inspires me to visit the library of the U.S. Department of Agriculture, where I find enough old newspaper articles to trace their introduction into this country.

Dr. C. C. Young, a Chicago dentist whose father and grandfather had raised Karakuls in Bessarabia, decided that he wanted to raise the sheep of the Russian nobility on his Texas farm. Apparently, he liked challenges.

In 1909, the emirate of Bokhara had been a semidependency of Russia for fifty years, and the Russian government, which controlled nearly the entire Karakul international fur trade, was fully aware of the value of the lambskins. One author states that a coat made of purebred Karakul pelts cost (in 1909) from $500,000 to $1 million.

Pure Karakul sheep were hidden on the farms of Russian noblemen and guarded by Cossacks. Foreigners could enter these fortresses only on permits granted by the war minister. Moreover, as Dr. Young learned, the sheep were considered sacred by the local Islamic tribes. They were not available to the "infidel."

Dr. Young persisted. Through a congressman, he appealed to President Theodore Roosevelt. This connection produced a letter of introduction to the Russian czar. But what really mattered was his contact with the former minister of agriculture, who knew how the system worked. The process dragged on, but eventually, the Poltava Agricultural Society approved Dr. Young's request. He would be permitted to take his three rams and twelve ewes to America. This was just the beginning.

He had the sheep driven on foot, *one thousand miles* through the desert to Libau, their Baltic Sea port of embarkation. The two-week transatlantic voyage may have seemed like a rest. But then the fifteen sheep were refused entrance into the United States. They were from Asia; undoubtedly they carried "all kinds of Asiatic diseases."

So Dr. Young went back to his Congressional allies. Just hours before the Karakuls were to be turned back to Bokhara, they were allowed to enter the United States on the condition that they undergo months of blood testing and other analyses. They all managed to survive these ordeals and eventually arrived at Dr. Young's Texas farm.

14

First Shearing

I'm making progress with closing our firm. I have now begun discussions with two of my clients about engaging other attorneys. This is serious. I wonder how I'll feel when their monthly retainer checks stop coming.

All the while, I like to believe that my faithful Saturdays and Sundays with the lambs have gained a certain amount of credibility with the breeder.

"Would you be willing to come down to my farm," I boldly ask, "to show us what you mean by all these connected paddocks?"

He takes a deep breath. "Okay, but it's time for them to be shorn." *Gulp*. More trauma. To be tossed around while a loud buzzing thing scrapes the wool off your body. It is unimaginably awful.

As it turns out, I am the only one who is alarmed. Lambs like

Rameau. I developed great respect for this small young woman and her electric shearing device, which was heavy and larger around than a beer can, vibrating and with extremely sharp blades. Rameau appears to be enjoying having his fleece removed. At this young age, his wool probably weighs about fifteen pounds. You can see his one little horn. The Karakul ram develops a beautiful display of horns. As my sheep were wethers, there were very few horns among them, and they were, like Rameau's, very small.

haircuts. They know when to yield and what to yield to. Today, they calmly allow me to practice my halter-leading skill. I am studiously tying one of them to a board fence when a young woman flounces in with a large canvas bag slung over her shoulder. She looks like she's arriving at a modern dance class. No greetings. She plops the sack on the ground, sweeps long bangs out of her eyes with a calloused hand, and commands the breeder to roll out her tarpaulin. She pulls out the shearing device, which looks like an oversize beer can, and oils the blades.

I am invisible until she says, "Okay, give me that first black one." The shearer cannot weigh much more than the six-month-old lambs, but she has been shearing sheep since she was a youngster. With total confidence, she rotates each lamb in one long contortion. She leans forward, and wool peels off the legs and the belly. Now she twists her back and with another smooth movement shaves the lamb's back. What looks like a fleece rug drops to the ground. A final cosmetic whisk around the chin and she sets the lamb on his feet. The breeder scoops up an armful of warm fleece and pushes it into the bag I hold open. Before I can tie it, she jerks her head toward me. "Hey! Pay attention. Gimme that white one. Okay. What do we have here? Is this a ram or a ewe?"

Some farmers say that once they are shorn, lambs are technically sheep. Others insist that they are lambs until they are a year old.

Mine will remain The Lambs.

15

New Farm Life

Weekends will never be the same. There are no more strolls down deserted Washington streets to my office. For so many years, I returned to Washington from client meetings in New York or Paris on Fridays so that I would have the entire weekend to get ready for the next week. Now I am doing my best to avoid long trips so that I can gather a few supplies and spend those days at the farm.

My friends worry that I will feel isolated. Wrong! I wonder if I will ever have any privacy. Someone is knocking on the front screen door all day long. My first uninvited visitor is the woman who owns the enormous farm on the other side of the stream. Her curiosity propels her to my door at eight o'clock on a Sunday morning. She asks, "Who are you and what are you doing here?"

One day, an elderly black man appears. He has grown up "just down the road from this here farm" and will help me in any way. The following week, he comes with a friend. Only minutes away, I have all the fencing, weed-spraying, and hay-mowing services I might ever need.

One Sunday morning, I venture into the small white frame church in the village. Robert E. Lee had tethered his horse to a tree in the churchyard when he visited during the Civil War. I might be tempted to join this church, but I'm wary. This is a small agricultural community with strong ties—or pretensions—to early Virginia. I'm an outsider, from a big city, and I have been warned by a neighbor that I will be suspect because of my foreign traveling. But thinking back to those many trips to Europe reminds me that all of that travel probably has a lot to do with my presence here.

I remember a conversation last year with a Belgian attorney friend who also has clients around the globe. I was going to be in Brussels for a monthlong project, and he had offered his guest suite to me. When I opened the bathroom medicine cabinet, I saw shelves crammed with soaps and shampoos from hotels all over the world. I found it disturbing.

At dinner that evening, he couldn't wait to tell me about an American attorney with whom he thought he had a romantic future. He wanted to settle down. Then I mentioned the soap collection. "That's just it," he said. "It's about all I have to show for decades of traveling." We agreed that it's almost impossible to have any kind of social life when people do not know where you will be from week to week. "They try, you know," he says. "But then, after a while, they give up. You think you're coming home, but you look through your phone messages and realize you have more friends in the city you just left."

My love of travel lingers from enchanted days when my mother took me along on her shopping trips to Seattle or San Francisco. Living in Montana, Seattle was considered "town." We would take our breakfasts from silver serving pieces in the dining car of beautiful trains. Those were the days when we would dress for the trip, always wearing hats and gloves.

My father would have ordered roses to fill her rooms. She would instantly order in tea, and we would plan our days of shopping, concerts, and museums. In the cities I regularly visit, my relationships with colleagues and hotels and churches persuade me that I have a worldwide home, not just my pretty yellow apartment on a tree-lined avenue in Washington.

But last summer, the miniature roses in a window box facing that pleasant street were so black from exhaust fumes that I felt like a murderer. I then filled a room with orchids. But as lovely as they are, they do not grow in legitimate soil. I grew up with real dirt on my hands. Perhaps I have been secretly longing to return to the little patch of lettuces and carrots that my grandfather once edged off for me.

16

Career

If I hadn't been tending my vegetables, I would have been reading my own little books about animals or fairies. People around me thought I was a prodigy because I could read these stories to them, but I had simply heard them so often that I had memorized them and knew when to turn the pages.

So important had my books been to me that on my college applications I declared my goal in life was to write books for children. I naturally studied English literature. When I won the *Mademoiselle* magazine writing contest, which allowed me to work as a college board editor for a year, I thought I had achieved my girlhood dream of becoming a writer. It was a thrilling year, contributing my observations of fashion trends on the Colorado ski slopes to a national magazine. My piano teacher appreciated my literary aspirations and begged me to go to New York to stay with her friend who worked for a major talent agency. I wasn't ready for that, but Parker's peacock blue ink, which I was using then, became the emblem of my writing career.

At the same time, a friend arranged a job for me at the new National Endowment for the Arts in Washington. We would be changing the course of the arts in America. I loved the work, meeting directors of orchestras and corresponding with famous choreographers. It took more than a year for me to recognize that as I was supporting other people's creativity, I'd forgotten my own. A future in arts administration did not challenge me. I was off my track.

I had lost the thread of my literary life, but I followed my love of books and research into my father's profession. Although I had no dreams of performing in courtrooms, I relished law school. I know my father was pleased. I would never have his ability to remember case details, but I was lured by the laws of other countries.

The University of Denver had one of the first programs in international legal education. Its director was one of those true educators who take great interest in each student. He guided us into internships or other schools, often writing letters of recommendation from his home at the weekend. One day he announced to me, "If you don't get out of Denver pretty soon, you're going to be terribly provincial."

When he suggested a program in Paris that would round out my knowledge of European tax systems, I was packed before I had filled out the applications. For the next three years I analyzed a lot of foreign inheritance and estate tax rules, but I also practiced on a piano that Maurice Ravel had played, walked to my classes through gardens designed in the late seventeenth century, and made friendships that will almost certainly last for the rest of my life.

Considering myself thoroughly internationalized, returning to the West was impossible. I found Washington, D.C., bland after Paris, but I thought it was a good base. I quickly learned that I was out of step to join an associate track in a large law firm. No one was impressed by my studies of foreign jurisdictions. But after a few months of tedious beginner's assignments in a small firm, I decided to test my luck on my own.

I would combine my love of the arts with my knowledge of foreign tax laws and pioneer a practice of guiding wealthy individuals in making tax-deductible contributions to foreign charities. Then, too, there was the possibility of working with corporations. Japanese companies were buying America. They knew nothing of our practice of corporate good citizenship. I would teach them.

"Oh, but the Japanese will not hire a woman," I would hear. "Oh, the Japanese don't go near boutique law firms." Or: "You will not live long enough to survive the courtship with a Japanese company." What no one knew is that by chance I would meet a seasoned Japan expert, a former ambassador, who thought my idea had merit. With his invitations to speak at the high-level business conferences he was organizing, I was able to launch a specialty practice that grew, steadily, until I had six colleagues working with me and a client list that included major multinational companies in Japan and Europe. Soon, in New York and Paris and Tokyo, I was accompanying clients to exhibitions and concerts they had underwritten with my guidance, and I was speaking at conferences around the world, where I was often the only American on the program.

One spring morning in Paris, the scent of the tiny green linden flowers in the air, I suddenly had the idea of inviting my father to join my firm. I can picture that moment so clearly: I am stepping off a curb when I think of him, with his white wavy hair and trim form, always in neatly tailored navy blue suits. Just the right gravity for my little firm and a bracing new challenge for him.

Everyone was thrilled. The Japanese clients revered him. One of them refused to work with anyone else. Together, we presented our subject at major international law congresses. Seasoned foreign lawyers were drawn to him, showering him with dinner invitations and begging him to join projects in Holland and Greece and Turkey. Some became close personal friends.

We joined the law reform initiatives in several former Communist countries. Our task was to draft new legislation for voluntary associations. What a thrill to invest our legal experience to promote a more peaceful world. My old law school professor declared, "It's time for you to write the book about all of this. I will introduce you to the best Dutch publisher." I met the Kluwer representative at a table in front of the florist's shop in the Hague train station.

It was a massive undertaking, gathering research from reporters in sixty-two countries, crafting summaries of rules and policies from English, which was often the second language. But I couldn't wait to get up at four o'clock to write for a few hours before going to my office. Even though I knew I was not producing a literary work, I still had my turquoise blue ink, which a new manufacturer had renamed *bleu des mers du sud*, and I had affirmed that I had the temperament for the discipline of writing. Composing the introduction was my reward for the entire project. I spent hours selecting the words to express my hope that this text would advance good works around the world. Way down inside me, the writing of those six pages registered.

17

The Lambs Arrive

After the excitement of the first shearing, it is time to get to work. Two of my neighbors ingeniously carry out the breeder's rough diagram for a series of temporary paddocks. With a dozen rolls of woven wire and a truckload of metal posts, they connect eight pens to a six-foot-wide central aisle, which leads to the water buckets and feed supply.

The small white frame horse shed is watertight and needs only a serious sweeping. It will be a comfortable sanctuary for thirteen lambs, its warm pine interior lit by a forty-watt ceiling lightbulb. Another neighbor arrives with a truckload of square hay bales, straw for bedding, and a fifty-pound sack of Prime Lamb 16, lamb baby food.

It is now late May, approaching one year since I first sat on the green bench with my father. He has traveled across the country for the momentous arrival of The Lambs. On the first evening, we toast his return. Not a mention of closing our firm. He is no more focused on that process than I am. This has nothing to do with any blurring of his mind or the quality of his memory. The business at hand has crowded every other concern out of our minds.

Tomorrow The Lambs will arrive! As I clear away our dinner dishes, I wonder if my dream of the spiral of translucent sheep will recur in some new variation.

The great day is here. By noon, a dozen friends have gathered. They organize silk quilts on the slope above the white shed. There are trays of fruits and baskets of fresh bread, and a healthy supply of champagne. Around one o'clock, the breeder parks next to the white shed. Under his camper cover, the pipe-curled heads of thirteen nine-month-old lambs press toward the back of the pickup.

The tailgate lowers, and Ginastera—in one great cinnabarine blaze—hops out. Bach, all café au lait, and India ink Saint-Saëns immediately follow, and then the others, in twos or threes, nimbly negotiate the three-foot drop. They don't land in a chaotic heap. They form a tight cluster, which gently pulsates while they gaze at the scene and at one another. They may be absorbing a new environment, but they betray not the slightest trace of timid "sheepishness."

While this fifteen-hundred-pound woolly mass assembles, the men spring into action. My neighbor passes two flakes of hay to my father. His blue eyes sparkle as he shakes them out into the glistening red hayrack. The breeder nudges the curly bodies through an opening in the wire pen. I stand perfectly still. I can feel a smile stretching across my face. My eye lights on the ruffled cuff of my white linen blouse, wholly unsuitable to a paddock and soon to be replaced by a cotton knit shirt. But today it is a vestment for an important ceremony.

Thirteen pairs of long ears point forward, tilting slightly down, as though they are listening for my voice. The Lambs stand straight, their narrow bodies lower over the shoulders, backs sloping upward toward flat, fat Karakul tails, most of which curl up at the tips.

I cannot stop looking at them. My own flock of sheep? How did this happen? Certainly I have forgotten my Washington apartment with its taffeta curtains and chintz-covered furniture. I have not the slightest remorse for missing a performance of the Baroque music group of which I am president.

My entire consciousness is fixed on the bouclé bodies facing me. Will they be happy here? Will they accept me? And what will they do tonight? Will they squeeze into the corner of their pen and bleat for the breeder as they cried for their mothers on that awful night of weaning? No, they are calm. They remain clustered together, but they seem to be enjoying themselves, standing alert but relaxed, sniffing their favorite molasses-laced grain pellets in the new red feed trough.

The fenced space is not broad enough for them to move in solid formation. They jauntily funnel out along both sides of the hayrack. They ignore their welcoming party.

Corks are popping. I catch fragments: "Her own flock of sheep." "How many people have a flock of sheep?" Friends from all over the world are dancing around in the apricot-tinted air. Meanwhile, The Lambs fall effortlessly into their established bunches. The twins, Saint-Saëns and Ginastera, stay together. The younger males huddle; the three ewe lambs are already inseparable.

I am an attentive hostess, but today my guests are on their own. I hear their happy burble and their applause when a guest arrives with a tire-size tray of sushi. They, too, are enjoying themselves, obviously capable of managing an improvised outdoor meal without my eminence. I am transfixed by what is going on in the pen, secretly wishing that one of The Lambs will come over to rub his head on my ankle.

The breeder hands me a fistful of black nylon halters and nods toward the pasture.

Oh, not now, I think. If they ever need to go to the vet, haven't the hours of practice given me the skill to get them into a truck? But this is great entertainment. Guests join in. I pull a harness over each little nose, and someone grabs the tether. Bach leads, holding his light brown head aloft like an Arabian stallion. Perfect composure. Then Ginastera and Saint-Saëns take turns prancing to the end of the paddock.

Halter training. *Whenever the breeder visited, I had to demonstrate my halter-training skill. The Lambs generally enjoyed the exercise—except Mozart, seen fourth from the left, straining against the lead.*

What if Mozart refuses to stand and I am the one who has to drag her all the way across the field in front of my party? But today she jerks her head around to let me know what she thinks of this bother and then mercifully cooperates. At the end of the exercise, Satie, who is decorated in great red polka dots on a white background, and the snow white one I have named Charpentier are small enough to perform together, led by a five-year-old boy.

Now the breeder declares that he cannot leave until I exhibit my hoof-trimming skill. Although Karakul sheep are famously resistant to foot rot, their hooves will have to be trimmed regularly for smooth walking. My father and a helper sit each lamb, one by one, on his rump. I open my shiny red hoof trimmers. The edges are razor sharp. I take care to trim very slightly. I suspect the breeder has already trimmed these hooves. "Now if you cut too deep and there is bleeding," he tells me, "you have to coat the foot with this disinfectant."

I misunderstand. There is not a drop of blood, but I douse all fifty-two feet in bluish green ink. My bright green fingers go to piano lessons and luncheons in Washington for the next two months.

As the sun spreads out into its pinks, reds, and violets toward the west and the guests pack up to leave, The Lambs wander into their new house. They gently jostle one another to find good places for the night. Saint-Saëns and Ginastera settle into one corner. Debussy edges Bach out of her way along the wall that she and Chopin will share with Mozart, who is already preparing a bed for herself in the two feet of loose straw. The younger males search out sleeping spots on the other side.

There is nothing impulsive about this process. They seem assured that there will be enough room for everyone. They simply make their claims, working around one another. Finally they are settled for the first night, and I am left to myself to try to sum up what has just happened to me. By now I am more or less reconciled to accepting everything around me here as unfamiliar, even though, at the same time, it is familiar, and I enter it less with the excitement of discovery than with the thankfulness of return.

18

Real Shepherdess

My nearest neighbor is recently retired and delighted to baby-sit The Lambs while I am in Washington a few days a week. "You'll be surprised how little care sheep need," he tells me. This is disappointing. I want to be a real shepherdess. But for now, he will maintain the little shed and the feed supply, and feed them in the morning and evening.

When I'm here, I march out smartly at eight o'clock for the morning feeding.

The door to the shed is a two-section Dutch door. Its lower half is about four feet high. Saint-Saëns, who is no more than twenty-four inches tall, quickly figures out that by planting his front feet on the rail of the lower section he can intercept every feed delivery. Day after day I encounter his triumphant face. He holds on tight, and it takes some maneuvering to get past him. With all four feet on the ground, he still thinks he deserves the first bite. This will always be part of the ritual.

Young lambs at the hayrack. The Lambs, about one year old in this picture of the twice-daily scene at the feed trough, have been shorn twice, and the early brilliant colors of their fleeces have faded. Ginastera, third from the left in the foreground, is no longer glistening copper, and even the solid black lambs have many gray hairs. Seven of the males are huddled in the front. On the far side, the three ewe lambs are together, as they almost always are. On the far left you see Mozart, solid black Chopin, and then Debussy. Mozart is not eating, presumably to maintain her exquisite figure.

Morning and evening, I place one flake of orchardgrass hay for each lamb in the top of the hayrack. The Lambs indifferently pull out strands of this hay. What matters to them is the red plastic scoop that serves their delicious protein-rich Prime Lamb 16, a concoction of molasses, processed corn, and barley seed. Anything from that scoop will always be a treat, even if it is reduced to low-calorie soy-hull pellets.

It is impossible to express the thrill of being surrounded by these compact woolly creatures. And while I can't say that they seem to be filled with childlike awe, they certainly do a great amount of looking around, as though they find delight in their new home. Every day here, as the mist rises off the pond to greet the sun, feels like a new beginning. Life is fresh. I am in the home that has been waiting for me all my life. And now, with The Lambs in place, it all feels so natural and so complete that I wonder how I had ever convinced myself that I wanted any other sort of life.

19

A New Home

Days of easing down into the farm follow. The stream completely captivates me. A few sections are too deep for me to see the bottom. Others stretch out into strips of shining earth-toned pebbles. Always the water is slow and lazy, with just enough movement to catch shadows and to whisper wordlessly. There are the gentle hillsides that rise to overlook the sycamores at its bank. Crows broadcast their morning demands from the treetops.

One day, I invite the local contractor to consult on enlarging the white shed to house fully grown sheep. I confess to him that what I'd really like to do is design my own barn. His eyes light up. The next thing I know, we are scouting around for a good site on the far side of the house. I prefer to leave The Lambs where they are. "Why don't we build a barn next to the little shed?" I ask. "It will be familiar. And don't forget that they're named for composers. The old piano ought to live in the barn. We can have concerts."

After I feed The Lambs in the morning, I follow them into one of the new paddocks. I sit on the ground, with my back against the wire fence. They quickly arrange themselves around me in what is now an established pattern. Bach, Ginastera, and Saint-Saëns stay to my left. Debussy stands directly in front of me. Chopin is next to her, and farther over, the other solid black male—the one who approached me at the breeder's farm—whom I have named Fauré. Mozart lies on the ground behind this formation. The younger ones stay beyond her.

Sitting on the ground, I am able to admire their very lean, fragile-looking legs. Karakuls (in the Turkic languages, *kara* means "black"; *kul* means "leg") typically have exquisite black legs. In my group, Debussy, Mozart, and Charpentier have white wool extending down from their white torsos. Ginastera, of course, has polished terra-cotta legs, and Bach's are light beige. All the others have ballet-dancer straight, narrow, typically Karakul black legs, which tempt me to wear black tights.

They work out a rotation for my attention. First, Ginastera comes for a caress. He's not shy about presenting his chin, which is covered in tiny tight baby curls. Then comes Bach. And then Saint-Saëns, who can never get too much affection and does not move away until Debussy nudges him aside. Then Chopin, and finally, Fauré. Everyone from the older group approaches except for Mozart, who is in her own world. The younger ones don't avoid me, but they don't seek attention.

The contractor is almost a daily visitor. He paces the area we have

Young sheep together in the pasture. (TOP) At the base of an old oak tree that became a favorite afternoon gathering place.

My father with the flock. (BOTTOM) A tight little flock wrapped around my father in the pasture just below the barn. The surrounding stream is hidden behind the dense belt of trees to the left, behind us. Charpentier, who is off to the right, often stayed in his own world.

identified for the new barn, takes photographs, and studies the different levels of the ground. He is ready to begin making rough drawings.

"Well, wait until I collect some pictures of French barns," I say. "If
we're going to make a little dream world here, we have to have a
French-inspired barn."

We agree to the general shape. The lower level, which will be
built into the hillside just below the house, will store equipment.
The ground floor will be for The Lambs. We'll also have an office and
a bathroom along one side, and space to store the piano in winter.
And we'll copy the high-pitched roof of old Normandy barns.

One morning, the contractor follows me into a paddock to admire
my flock. Bach, who stands in front, yanks back his head, stiffens
his neck, and dramatically stamps his front left foot. "What was that
about?" I ask.

"Well, as I've told you, I don't know anything about sheep," he
replies, "but I know from a few hunting trips that with deer, the one
in front will stamp his foot if a stranger comes too close. It isn't so
much to stop the person. It's a signal to warn the ones behind him."

In the afternoons, I return to The Lambs. Sometimes they continue
to search around for delicacies such as clover. I am able by now to
recognize their grazing pattern. Two heads are always up—on
the alert—while the others bend to nip the grass. This afternoon,

Debussy and Bach are watching. Sentries regularly rotate. As Bach bends his head toward the ground, Ginastera and Saint-Saëns lift theirs. This is an advantage of living in a flock. The more sets of eyes, the less time anyone needs to look out for motion in the distance. Saint-Saëns keeps a constant eye on me. I learn to take note of his approach. It can easily cost a shoelace or a page out of a book.

Most afternoons, after a morning of gulping down as much grass as they can process during a period of rumination, The Lambs arrange themselves in a tight cluster on the ground. The Karakul is said to be an unusually tight-flocking breed, and, in this first year, they proceed through the fields in one mass. The older ones lead; the younger ones trade places along the rim.

Most days, I am alone here. I want nothing more than to absorb this land into myself. I begin to sense its rhythms. I listen for the morning polyphony of birds, which fades into the quiet of late afternoon. My skin waits for changes in the air from morning to evening.

Light plays a part. As a stream of sunlight flows out over a stack of boulders, the green moss on their surfaces turns yellow. An intense morning beam transforms a dead tree into an ebony statue; at noon, the sun will refract its nude branches into diaphanous plumage. Early-evening light filters over the barn excavation until even the most violent gouges of the bulldozer are as smooth as young faces.

20

If Today Be Sweet

I 've been here for just over a year, and by now my father has instituted a routine of regular visits. He never mentions all those days
we spent together with clients in New York, London, or Athens. He
doesn't seem to want to talk about his favorite bookstores around
the world. Oh, but how I look forward to his visits. I invest myself
in these breaks for him, into his "poetry country" of pastures and
new friends and, of course, The Lambs. To see the smile on his face
as he steps out of the car fills me with joy. He looks around like a
child who cannot decide what to do first.

Any other visitor would arrive complaining about the trip all the
way from Montana. His first flight leaves Helena at six in the morning. Then there is the waiting in Salt Lake City and a five-hour flight
across the country. After that, he can expect at least two hours by
car in rush-hour traffic. But he was always a skilled traveler, and
none of this matters. Within minutes he swaps his traveling suit for

green corduroy pants and a threadbare tweed jacket. "Well, honey, I suppose I am a little weary, but, well, how about another little drop of wine?

"What I thought I'd do tomorrow is start taking apart those old railroad tie stairs behind the house." Then he tells me he's not terribly hungry, before devouring everything on offer.

"That's the spirit," I say, encouraging him as he drains the wine bottle into his glass. "Well, Daddy, you've had a long day. Why don't we get you settled for a good night in the country silence."

"Oh, that sounds wonderful," he says, "but before I go down to my room, I thought you'd like to see this."

He reaches into his bag for a large book, Robin Lane Fox's masterful volume, *The Search for Alexander*. I was wondering how long it would be before he felt compelled to dive into ancient Persia. With a lifetime of reading into the antiquity of Greece and the Middle East, he can hardly wait to investigate the history of The Lambs. "You know, don't you, that the area where they come from is truly ancient? It's Uzbekistan now, but when Alexander the Great conquered it, it was called Sogdiana. Balkh, one of the oldest cities in civilization, is just across the current border in what is now Afghanistan. It was Alexander's eastern capital for a time."

The vision of ancient Persia overtakes him. Momentarily forgetting any tiredness, he recites a few lines from Omar Khayyám:

> *Ah, fill the Cup: what boots it to repeat*
> *How Time is slipping underneath our Feet:*
> *Unborn To-morrow, and dead Yesterday,*
> *Why fret about them if To-day be sweet!*

And with that, he goes off to dream of the romance of Persia: roses and nightingales in elegant gardens, fast horses, mysterious women, sharp sabers, carpets with colors glowing like jewels, poetry, and melodious music.

The very word *paradise* is from the Persian *paradaida*, what the Persian called his beautiful park, everything to delight in: the beauty of the trees, the perfect accuracy with which they had been planted in straight lines, the exquisite scents that mingled together to fill the air.

As soon as I clear away our dinner dishes, I cannot resist *The Search for Alexander*. I'm too weary for any serious reading, but when the book falls open to a central two-page image of a remarkable ruin, I have my first glimpse of King Darius's Persepolis.

What remains of this structure is a wide stairway leading up to a vast limestone platform. Row upon row of figures representing soldiers and courtiers—subjects from all over the empire—line the stair wall, frozen into stone relief. Soon I will learn that these frieze figures along the East Apadana Stairway represent Persians and Medes, Indians and Egyptians, Babylonians and Greeks, all of whom are bringing offerings to Darius, the King of Kings, in an annual demonstration of homage and loyalty.

But wait! One pair of subjects is presenting two lambs to him. My eyes widen as I look at their tails. These are fat-tailed sheep! Before long, I will learn that production of the prized Karakul lambskins in Bokhara and Khiva has been documented in records dating back to 978 B.C. I will discover that in the 1930s, the German Archaeological

Society, in its excavation of the Anatolian site Zincirli, had found Karakul-trimmed jackets that had been worn by Hittite kings. And I still believe that if I search long enough I will find evidence that the costly lambskins were among the merchandise for which T'ang dynasty Empress Wu—wearing her legendary silk robes woven without seams—bribed the nomads with intoxicating liquors.

My father has arrived with more than a bag of books. He has also made a list of tasks for himself. He has discovered shreds of rusted barbed wire around trees along the stream, and one project is to gather this nasty stuff. By the end of the week, there will be a heap of old barbed-wire rolls as large as my car.

But my father has apparently been doing more than rolling up scraps of barbed wire. He has cultivated a special relationship with Satie, the youngest and smallest lamb, the white one with great blotches of copperish red on his sides. Whenever I see my father with The Lambs, Satie is beside him. Satie has not so much as acknowledged my presence, and yet he maintains almost constant physical contact with my father. Look at the group wrapped around him now. Focus on the center of the scene, the man in the tattered jacket and old wool hat. Train your eyes on the man's left hand. In his palm you will see the slender red and white snout of Satie.

One afternoon, my father is sitting beside me on a rock in the pasture with The Lambs. He calls my attention to how rhythmically they move toward and away from us. "Now you watch how they go out," he suggests as they spread into the field. "But it won't be long

Satie and his best friend. Satie attached himself almost like an appendage to my father. If you saw one of them, you could depend upon seeing the other one.

until they come back to check in." It is as though they have mutually
agreed to this movement.

Before the leaves tarnish to rust, the contractor comes to discuss an
apartment for my father in the new barn. He asks me, "Don't you
think he needs his own space, since he seems to be almost a permanent resident?"

"Well, let's ask him," I reply. We have a long, easy conversation over
the possibilities for a special guest room. The contractor proposes an
area nestling under the thick roof beams. "It might be just a little
inconvenient to come down the flight of stairs to use the bathroom."

I'm surprised to hear my father's response. "It sounds wonderful.
It would be like heaven to sleep so close to The Lambs. I suppose it
would be all right for the time being. But I wonder about the years
ahead. It might be difficult to handle the steps." As far as I can remember, this is his first admission of the challenges of age. He has
repeatedly assured me that he knows how to pace himself. I have
watched him take his time in lifting things and even walking up the
slopes here. I register this statement.

21

Le Berceau

I haven't given any thought to a name for the farm until one morning when I am strolling down the lane and the French word for lullaby, *berceuse*, comes alive in my mind. It stays with me all morning, until I take the hint. Of course. A *berceau* is a cradle, an oblong-shaped place of safety and containment.

In looking up the word, I learn that, in older French, a *berceau* was an arbor, much like the scene of the lane, with branches meeting overhead, sunlight filtering through. As though it had always had this name, the farm becomes Le Berceau. A tranquil enclosure, the place of dreams.

By the middle of frozen January, the barn is almost finished. It is a dark creamy chestnut construction. Across the front are white-trimmed French windows with graphite gray shutters. The roof is a magnificent feat: steeply pitched and then curved to crawl out over ground-floor rooms along both sides. A terra-cotta-tiled pent roof—

an affordable hint of Provence—covers the entrance; yard-long iron strap hinges span the huge front doors. The central room is a vast pine cavern. Massive king-post trusses support a ceiling that looks fifty feet high. If it weren't so apparently rustic, it would evoke the grandeur of a cathedral. The finishing touch is eight large "antiqued" Louis XV–style wall lights that I found in New York.

The Lambs huddle around me on the porch of the house as the bulldozer growls up the road. We watch it demolish their white home, which is blocking the entrance to the new barn. A couple of sturdy taps, and the shed, like a trampled dollhouse, rides in the bucket to a fire pit in a bottom field. But the barn is not quite ready for The Lambs, and they will take up residence on the flagstone terrace of the house.

I picture myself in one of those old houses in Europe or the Middle East whenever I step out onto a thick bed of straw. The Lambs look up from contentedly eating their hay out of two wicker chairs or from simply eating the chairs.

Unfortunately, they leave a four-inch-thick residue of moisture and straw. I call it adobe. The contractor calls it concrete. "It'll take us days to get this stuff out of here," he grumbles. Two of his carpenters throw themselves at the task with heavy steel digging bars. They want to use dynamite. I mention my fantasies of sleeping there with The Lambs on hot summer nights. The contractor does not smile. "No. Miss George, I want you to promise me this one thing. They are *not* going to be living on that stone terrace, because we are not going to clean up this mess again."

Residence on the terrace. The Lambs' white shed had to be demolished in order to accommodate the huge front doors of the barn. For a few days, they were installed on the terrace of the house, amusing themselves by eating the wicker chairs, which were used as hayracks.

One cool spring morning, the piano mover comes with a dolly to roll the old piano into the barn. Ginastera, Saint-Saëns, and Bach are practically on his heels. I follow. Poulenc (who will be the self-appointed trough monitor) begins an inspection of the wooden feed troughs. Debussy smacks her rump against Bach's side as they jostle each other into what will be their assigned mealtime positions at the front interior hayrack.

Ginastera, who has never been in the presence of a piano, immediately zooms underneath to scratch his back on its moisture-

control device. Satie and Charpentier wander out into the run-in to claim one exterior hayrack. This will be their corner, where they will hollow out shallow cradles in the packed soil.

Now the concern is to find bedding places along the walls. Bach stakes out the spot between his feed trough and the run-in door. Debussy settles at the center of the back wall. To her right, Saint-Saëns and Ginastera share the corner beside the feed closet. The young ones cluster along the wall outside the office. Once claimed, these spaces are inviolable.

Weeks fly by, and suddenly I am aware of real summer warmth in the morning air. On clear days like today, while The Lambs finish eating, I like to sit at the small marble-topped table on my father's

Poulenc. (ABOVE LEFT) For Poulenc, there could never be too much of anything. As soon as The Lambs were installed in the barn, he appointed himself as the manager of the feed troughs. What this meant was that after everyone else had finished eating, he began a thorough collection of every last grain pellet. As you can readily see in this image, he does not appear to have missed many meals. **View into run-in from barn interior.** (BELOW LEFT) This picture is taken from the large interior room of the barn, the primary home of The Lambs. You can just barely make out the shape of the hayracks on either side of the door into the run-in. Below each hayrack is a wooden feed trough. There are two other hayracks on the other side of the wall, in the run-in area, which gives onto the large security pen. After our initial experiment with connecting fenced areas, all the fences except this one were taken down. We had no close neighbors, we very rarely heard a dog barking in the distance, and we felt completely safe in our pastoral refuge, where we spent our days in the embrace of nature, fearing no evil.

loft balcony. Shaded here, I can sip a cup of tea while I marvel at the palette of greens at the stream's edge. Huge maples at one end sway in the breeze. White sycamore trunks flicker in fresh morning light.

Below me, The Lambs leisurely arrange themselves to endure another one-hundred-degree day. One front leg bends onto the knee joint, then the other, and finally the body sinks onto one side. High heat does not arrive in one great blast. First the sun slides across the pond. By eleven o'clock, it is huge and pulsing. It smashes down on us slightly after midday. But tea on the shaded balcony is a stolen moment to observe changes on the ground, and I know that below me my lambs are settled as well as possible to survive the warm weather. It is hot, but this is summer in Virginia, and there is not a single way in which life could be improved.

Ginastera. (ABOVE RIGHT) Ginastera is standing at the side doors of the barn. Behind him is the doorway of the barn office. This heated section of the first floor was the winter home of the old piano, which was typically in the center of the main room. The golden walls were painted using powdered pigment that I carried home in plastic bags from the ocher hills of the South of France. The powder was mixed with linseed oil to produce this rich color. If required a very long drying time, for which The Lambs had absolutely no patience.
Charpentier. (BELOW RIGHT) Charpentier, framed in the front window of the barn, The Lambs' new home. The large front doors were open most of the time, and they freely went in and out.

22

Rameau

Just outside the run-in, one of the youngest lambs is lying on the ground, apart from the group, violently rocking, as though he is struggling to stand, craning his neck over his left shoulder. Exactly what the breeder had warned me of. I am new to my life as a shepherdess, but I know without question that this lamb is dying.

I run to telephone the breeder. Feed him yogurt, I'm told, just to give him some nourishment. I have no idea how to get yogurt into him, and anyway, there is no yogurt in the house. I take out the telephone directory to locate a vet.

I have heard that no vets are interested in sheep. What farmer troubles with a vet when he factors the annual loss of a certain percentage of his flock to disease, age, or predator? Veterinary schools do not even bother teaching sheep medicine. I go down the list of large-animal vets.

"No, we handle only cattle."

"No, we specialize in horses."

"No, thank you, we do not treat sheep."

"But I feel certain that he's dying," I say.

"Even more reason why we won't come."

And there he lies. By now, his black eyes are glassy. He thrusts his head over his left shoulder. Is he trying to show me where he hurts?

Finally, late in the day, one vet, after protesting that he handles only horses and cattle, warns, "Hey, look, I've tried to tell you I don't know anything about sheep. . . . Okay, okay, give me half an hour." I am so comforted by his presence that I overlook his reference to my pet lambs as "culls." He swaggers into the barn in worn-out cowboy boots, jeans torn at the knees, red suspenders over a plaid shirt.

"Like I tried to tell you on the phone . . ." He admits he has no idea what the problem might be. His only suggestion is that I build an enclosure for Rameau in the barn, just inside the run-in doors. He will feel secure there, separated from the others by no more than a sheet of woven wire. My kind neighbor hammers slats for a low fence. I spread straw on the floor for a bed. A stack of hay bales is a table for a bowl of grain and a pan of water. I already know the outcome, but I cannot stop thinking, Oh, if only he'll eat, we might have a chance. He eats nothing.

The next morning, the vet stops by. "He's got to eat. I know this much about sheep. That stomach system requires something in it."

The next day, Doc tells me to force food and liquid into him. I am to squeeze a mixture of cooked oatmeal and water into his mouth with a device that looks like a turkey baster. With that, I begin my sad morning and evening ritual of walking up the bare dirt slope to my house—this is before the lawn has been planted—to prepare a pot of cooked oatmeal that has to be gotten into this poor creature. I know I will never again eat cooked oatmeal.

Revolting as this is, two days later, Rameau is standing in his pen! The oatmeal glop might be working. My faithful neighbor helps me lead him for a little walk. He eagerly steps out in front of the barn. I clean under his tail, although I wonder whether his skin is now especially tender due to his affliction. But he stands patiently. What do we do next? Well, back to his little prison until Doc comes tomorrow morning. The others hang their heads over the dividing wire. They observe, eyes wide and ears forward. We fence them inside the run-in to keep them close to Rameau.

Later that week, Rameau refuses to get up. I stay hopeful because, when I release the flock for a brief walk, he jerks forward and emits a low growl, as if to beg them not to abandon him. Is this a signal that he still wants to be part of his flock? But I cannot erase that first scene, when I knew deep inside myself that he was dying. Why am I prolonging this agony? I stay with Rameau the rest of the morning.

Suddenly, I realize that this is the first time I've ever had the sole responsibility for an animal's life. Of course, I fed my childhood puppy. But when he ran into the road and was hit by a car, my mother swiftly took over his burial in the garden, and before I could even feel sad, we were discussing piano lessons with the teacher who would become one of my most cherished friends. When I went off to law school, my two barely domesticated cats, Truffaut and Fellini, took up highly appropriate careers as barn cats in Montana.

Unbelievably, we continue our routine into the second week. I must be hypnotized. Oatmeal in the morning, fresh straw, fresh water. No more walking. Daily visits from Doc. Tenth day. No progress. Not one pellet of grain missing from his bowl. His eyes cloud. Twelfth day, and Rameau does not move. Forcing that tube into his throat is unbearable. Until last week, I've managed to persuade myself that I have wrapped the curtains of the world around this little farm and that everything will continue just as I've envisioned it. But my perfect paradise has been reconfigured as effortlessly as the turn of a hand rearranges the glass fragments of a kaleidoscope. I'm angry. I'm angry at the situation. I'm angry with the vet. I'm angry with poor motionless Rameau.

Mostly, I am angry with myself for going along with the charade of the past two weeks.

I tell myself I am prepared to face the decision that is glaring at me today. After feeding The Lambs, I walk up to the highest place on the ground. Here, across the road from the forest, is a sparsely wooded area overlooking the turn in the stream where it leaves to join the Rapidan River. When my neighbor arrives to help with Rameau, I ask him if he has time to open a grave in the dark red earth.

The vet arrives. There is nothing more to do. He states—I believe for his convenience—that he prefers to inject the overdose of a sleep-inducing drug at the burial site.

The men order me to leave. I step into the barn to spend a little time with Rameau. I feel like I am carrying him on my back as I slowly walk up the slope to my house.

I look out the upstairs window onto a scene that will haunt me. Rameau stands at the tailgate of the neighbor's truck, waiting to be heaved into its bed to go to his grave. Every part of him sags. His belly almost touches the ground. His head hangs. Even his ears look limp. An autopsy reveals that Rameau's stomach had burst and that a reservoir of the oatmeal slop had been collecting inside his distended skin. I will have that on my conscience forever.

It is four o'clock in the afternoon of the last Wednesday of July, almost two years since I first came to this place. Hot. My neighbor rests his arms on his shovel after filling in Rameau's grave. I kneel to arrange thirteen white roses on the bare earth. Together we read the Twenty-third Psalm. After he leaves, I return to the barn. An overwhelming loneliness drapes over me. Every detail of what I have accepted as a background scene now flies into my face with such force that years later I will remember the shadows from the side of the barn, the variations of light on the hillside, and the folds in my black leather skirt when I sat down on the grass beside the run-in. As soon as I lean onto my left forearm, Saint-Saëns collapses onto it. He's heavy. The last thing I need now is a broken arm. But I get his message: *Hey. We're still here and we've got a lot of things to do together.* The scent of lanolin that rises off his warm skin is a balm to my spirit.

We are together in the arms of nature. Nature can be cruel, and nature is sometimes harsh, but nature does not judge. Nature simply changes. The wound will leave a scar, but it will heal.

I set up a cassette player in the barn, and with The Lambs hovering around me, I listen to Rameau's music. The purity and gaiety of his "Gavotte Variée" lift me just a few inches above the events of the past weeks. As the shadows lengthen, I feel an overwhelming sense of belonging to this place and to these creatures. The music ends, and I sit in the darkness, knowing that even though I had the presentiment that Rameau would not live, still we had moments of hope, and we thought we were doing our best for him. And now I must forgive the old vet, and forgive the situation, and, most of all, forgive myself.

23

Entertainments

The summer is hot, but before long, the evenings are cooler, the days are shorter, and October approaches. It is time for fall shearing, and we will make it a festival.

To old friends and former colleagues from New York and Washington and Europe, Le Berceau is already an exotic novelty. The lady who goes to India to study miniature painting wants to come, and an adventurous pair who have ridden a bus into Mongolia invite themselves for this event.

We risk champagne glasses in the barn and gather around to marvel at the shearer's performance. Before anyone can snap a photograph, she whirls a lamb around. Zip and zip, down legs and a little tidying of the face, and on to the next one. My job is to bag the wool to go to a processor in Michigan. It is slightly surprising to find a few strands of gray among black fibers.

Waiting for haircuts. *Shearing became an important occasion, generally followed by a feast for invited guests and very often a piano recital in the barn while The Lambs resorted to head butting to reestablish their hierarchy. When the sound of two skulls colliding became unbearable, the sound of the piano was an immediate distraction. Ginastera would lunge under the piano to rub his back on the moisture-control device.*

Even Mozart relaxes into the shearer's arms, as though she is in a fancy hair salon.

Then the fun begins.

As soon as the shearing is finished, The Lambs begin to butt heads. All that quivering bare flesh is disturbing. But the woodblock *thunk* of two thick skulls is alarming. Don't they feel relieved to have all of that heavy, scratchy wool off their backs? Why the fighting?

Favorite afternoon music. The Lambs listened to my daily piano practice, either in the barn or lying on the grass outside the music room. They had definite taste in music. They were always content with the music of Mozart and Debussy, or Bach, or Chopin. But as soon as I ventured into the discords of Ginastera, they simply stood up and walked to the other side of the house. Their favorite source of music was the Cambodian *khloy* that my dear friend Ambassador Sichan Siv played for them. I often wondered whether the Asiatic sounds resonated deep in their memories. As long as Sichan was breathing into his wooden flute, they stayed as close to him as possible.

The shearer explains that they recognize one another by the scent carried in the fleece. Without their wool, the political hierarchy falls apart, and combat is sometimes needed to reestablish order. "But there's blood around Bach's horn," I cry.

She groans. "Come on. It's normal. Can't you see their skulls are built for it?"

Not only are their skulls built for it; there are no sharp points on their horns to inflict slash wounds. Over the millennia, sheep have developed very refined rules of combat. They fight just enough to settle their grievances. Afterward, there is no need for revenge and no lingering resentment.

The conflict itself is as choreographed as a fencing match in a ballet. Two square off. Very decisive eye contact seems to be the challenge to a duel. Then they simultaneously lower their heads. I suspect this may be an instinctual behavior to display the relative size of their horns. If so, it is interesting, since my males are wethers and their horns were arrested almost at birth. (The only horns in the group are Ginastera's little one-inch nubs, Bach's one three-inch horn, and Charpentier's single horn, which is about four inches long.)

Now each combatant takes a few steps back. After a second significant eye contact, each one turns his head ever so slightly to the right. And then the blow! It is as fierce as lightning. Again they back apart and size each other up. If additional combat is required, it is less vigorous. Usually two or three strikes are enough to preserve the stability of their society.

There is one sure way to bring the head butting to an end. If I go into the barn to play the old piano, within minutes our own barnyard rendition of a gamelan takes shape. Ginastera skids underneath to rub his back so vigorously that he has the piano rocking. Bach rubs his side against its flank while Saint-Saëns gnaws on a leg. Satie pounds his chin on the lowest keys. This is not exactly one of the concerts I'd envisioned, but it convulses our guests in laughter.

While I go off to prepare a lavish shepherd's pie (without lamb), my guest who comes with his Cambodian *khloy* in his pocket takes over with a more serene distraction. The Lambs love him and the sound of his hollow wooden melody, and they quickly arrange themselves in one long queue to follow him all through their pasture network.

When he sits on a rock outcrop to breathe his mysterious line into the air, The Lambs crowd around with their ears tilted forward, listening while his song springs aloft in patterns of Asian complexity. Shy Fauré is so captivated by these sounds that he uncharacteristically pushes his way to the front of the group. He is listening to the music that comes out of this wooden pipe; he has never approached the man.

24

Centering

And again, the following summer, during one stay in the course of a lazy June weekend, my Cambodian friend gathers The Lambs. His wife and I follow the happy band as they move into the pastures. No more than a hundred feet from the barn, Fauré stumbles. He slows his pace, and then he stops. Slowly, he turns away from the others, forgoing his beloved music and returning to the security of the run-in.

I spend most of the evening sitting beside him. He accepts a few bits of grain from my hand. He seems weak, but he isn't doing any of that awful neck twisting.

The next morning, he doesn't even try to stand. He turns his head away from a handful of feed. I wait. All that day, he refuses food, even water. The vet advises me, "Give it one more day."

No! Here is a lamb who won't get off the ground and who refuses to eat. Do I want more torture on my conscience? I do not answer to this vet. I know my lambs better than anyone else does. I do not hesitate, and Fauré will not suffer.

"No. Now." The vet begrudgingly concedes. There is no banter today. No talk of carrying a sick lamb to the cemetery. Fauré is the one who pressed his little head against my right ankle during that first remarkable afternoon at the breeder's farm. Now, after living here with me for two years, that curly black head rests on my right foot as Fauré drifts into oblivion.

Later in the month, the tall elegant representative of a French corporation invites me to lunch in Washington. We are members of a French business group, and I assume we will be planning a social event. That, however, is not his purpose. Sitting there in the dining room of a prestigious Washington club, he informs me that he has been diagnosed with a rare form of liver cancer and doesn't have much longer to live. He summarizes his trips to the Mayo Clinic and the plans he has made for his wife and three small children.

But what he especially wants to do is tell me about a form of meditation that a priest at the National Cathedral has taught him. Without centering prayer, he says, he would not be able to make all of his arrangements calmly. He tells me that he has the idea that anyone who goes off to live with lambs might appreciate knowing about it. Before we part, he mentions that the cathedral is planning a workshop on the technique, and he recommends a book.

In *Open Mind, Open Heart*, Father Thomas Keating refers to contemplative prayer as the "great therapist." If we can calm ourselves

Fauré. By now, Fauré's ink black coat has faded to a purplish gray. I will always remember his India ink black wool when I first saw him at the breeder's farm. Just before I left that afternoon, Fauré tentatively approached me, slowly moving toward my right leg. Then he lowered his curly little black head and rubbed it against my ankle. It was the first physical contact that one of them made with me, and it is unforgettable.

and wait to be "prayed through," he says, we will gradually examine our lives, shed unnecessary behaviors and people that are no more than habits, and discover our true selves.

I have often wondered why I found this attractive. Perhaps I was intrigued by the aspect of silence. Claude Debussy had said that he drew his music out of the reservoir of silence within himself. It is possible that the intervals of contemplation appeal to me

as condensations of my solitary daily life with the land and with
The Lambs.

⌒

In the seminar, many people complain that they do not have two
periods of twenty minutes in their days for such a practice. But I'm
outside the world of billable hours, or appointments, or even wrist-
watches. My life is governed by the dictates of the weather and the
feeding times for The Lambs, and centering prayer slips naturally
into the beginnings and closings of my days.

To consciously stop thinking is a challenge. But gradually I am
aware of my mental activity and how often my mind is going over
past events or planning for the future. In trying to empty my mind,
I become sensitive to each moment. I open my eyes with the sweet-
est refreshment. I look forward to these voluptuous periods of alert
receptivity as relief from worries, or projects, or even thoughts.
Meditation is about getting in touch with one's deepest truth, and I
like to believe that centering prayer gives me a taste of the state in
which The Lambs live their lives. They are nothing but expressions
of their essential natures. They draw their animal vitality and freedom from their capacity to live in the immediate moment. No resentment, no sorrow, no fear hunt down creatures who exist in the
eternal present.

Part Two

VOCATION

Living Out the Call

25

"They Know Your Voice"

"Y ou know, honey, I've been thinking. . . ."

"Yes, Daddy?"

"I think it's time to take The Lambs down to the pond."

"Are you serious? What about the forest?" I ask. "The bank of the stream isn't even fenced."

"Well, you have to trust them. Watch. They'll follow you. They know your voice."

My father has returned for a long stay. His stated purpose is to finalize details of closing our firm before the next annual meeting. I suspect he has his designs on the enormous closet of bookshelves in the loft bedroom. (I am thinking of the stack of cartons marked BOOKS that arrived at the village post office last week.)

But today, yes, is perfect for an adventure. The sky is calm under high clouds. It is the first day to want a sweater. My father unpacks a patched tweed jacket that looks like a relic from his university days. He has added a wild-turkey feather to the band of his old wool hat.

The Lambs mill around in the paddock next to the run-in. "Let's not herd them back through the barn doors," he suggests. "They're all here. We'll find a seam in the fence." Carefully, he pries open the wire ends. The Lambs bunch together, suddenly on the alert. Necks straighten, heads pull back, and ears jut forward.

We roll back about eight feet of fencing. The Lambs press themselves into one solid mass, just as they did on the day they arrived. They are so crowded around him that he has to lift his hawthorn walking stick over his head in order to move.

Onward toward the pond, one blur of animal motion eases down the slope to the bottomland. It is easy to see their hierarchy. Ginastera and Bach lead. Saint-Saëns tries to stay with the group but cannot resist a low branch of fading maple leaves. Debussy, Chopin, and Mozart stay close to me.

My father with Satie. (ABOVE RIGHT) *You have to imagine the look of adoration that Satie and my father exchanged in this image. My father did nothing to initiate Satie's affection; Satie selected him, and that was that.*
First visit to the front pasture. (BELOW RIGHT) *This image marks a major occasion. The Lambs had never been outside the space immediately around the house or in the lawn area between the barn and the house. But my father wanted all of us to go down to the front pasture, beyond the forest and completely out of the sight of the barn, to where the workers were clearing hundreds of scrub trees from the field. He insisted that The Lambs knew my voice and would stay with me. That day, Saint-Saëns began his practice of nipping low leaves from trees. Ginastera displayed his celebratory leaps into the air. The special adventure of this first visit to the front pasture became a daily ritual.*

My father follows, surrounded by the cluster of younger lambs, Satie glued to his side. Slowly, we process into the open front pasture, where my neighbor and his helper are rhythmically sawing scrub pines and hickories. The helper tells me, "You missed the truckloads of dead vines we pulled off the trees over at the stream. And there was a lot of old barbed wire down in the sand. We couldn't let Mr. George tackle that." Without masses of underbrush, I can see the very tall old trees standing as majestically as statues.

The Lambs do not hesitate. They lunge at the piles of logs. They yank dead leaves off branches as though it's something they've done every day. One heap of tree trunks is large enough for Ginastera to climb. Satie stays with my father.

Three carpenters, who have come to attach hardware to the folding wooden doors inside the barn, veer off the road to tell me how glad they are to see that Saint-Saëns and Ginastera are entertained and will not have their noses in the saws. My neighbor picks up his chain saw, and The Lambs and I continue to the three-foot-wide feeder stream that marks the front property line. Slightly more than three years ago, I crossed this threshold for the first time, and now here I am, back at this point with a flock of sheep. We then follow the edge of the stream all the way back toward the barn.

All of a sudden, Ginastera leaps off the ground. At two hundred pounds, he is no longer a gamboling young lamb, but something has thrust him four feet into the air. Is it the clean, crisp fall air, the rich aroma of pine and hay, or just his plain love of life? Poised in midair, he contorts his body. Then he lands, shakes his red head, and runs ahead of us, his heavy woolly tail flopping against his rump.

As we enter the barn, I smile. My father seems a little smug about the adventure. He has lived carefully, but has always known when to accept a challenge. He has correctly judged The Lambs. I hear his words: "Watch. They'll follow you. They know your voice." For some reason, the dream sheep come into my mind. Were they simply waiting for me to call them, to invite them into my life? I had never thought of that.

Then I ask myself another question.

Whose voice do I follow? And another question seems to come out of the blue: What happened to my writing ambitions? I had followed my father's footsteps into a career that was rewarding in many ways, but I had been listening to his voice and ignoring mine. But that little youthful voice was never completely silenced. Instead of taking up my pen, I have lived in the biographies of my favorite lady writers, Edith Wharton, Virginia Woolf, Vita Sackville-West, Edith Sitwell, Iris Origo, and spent hours looking down into the lines of Rilke and Hölderlin and Gerard Manley Hopkins. There is my shelf of notebooks, which I have filled with phrases and words from their works. In a moment of discouragement, I have only to take out a copy of "The Death of the Moth," and instantly my mood lifts when I ask myself for the hundredth time, How did she do that?

No, the voice has always been whispering, and I have always heard it.

26

Daily Circuits

The following morning, we take another walk down to the pond. And the next day, and the next. After a week, a daily practice is established: At eight o'clock, I present a scoopful of Prime Lamb to Saint-Saëns, who rushes to me. Then everyone else gets one big gulp. I distribute the hay in the four hayracks. The Lambs pull out a few mouthfuls before they begin to assemble at the front of the barn. By half past eight, they are in formation, Ginastera leading, all heads pointed toward the large doors, ready to go.

I often use their ability to predict the time of day as evidence of their intelligence. Perhaps it is not so surprising if one considers migrations and pregnancies and seasons and the constant need to anticipate the movements of predators. Konrad Lorenz states that animals would not survive if they didn't have the ability to think about how long an event would last or when it might recur, if they lacked sufficient memory to anticipate the order of a probable

Ginastera. We had known all along that Ginastera had leadership abilities. But once we instituted that daily morning walk down to the front pasture, he quickly rose to the occasion and, without any discussion or head butting, took up his position at the front of the group. Bach fell in behind him, and Saint-Saëns, who had no interest in politics, followed Bach even though he rarely lost sight of his twin brother, Ginastera.

train of events, or if they were unable to adjust to altered circum-stances.

Often I have been asked, "But what do you do during these walks?" So intimate is this time that I am tempted to reply that I don't do anything. These hours are the most precious part of the day, and I never take them for granted. To move at the pace of The Lambs or to sit while they graze allows me to see the details on the ground. This morning, for example, I watch a ladybug climb a leaf of grass. These are the luxuries that cannot be bought.

During these daily walks, I begin to learn The Lambs' ways. I notice that they do not entirely lift their rear legs off the ground.

Their back legs do not fully bend, and their feet drag across the terrain. Ginastera, Saint-Saëns, and Bach always press toward the front of the group. The three ewes and the younger ones generally lag behind or wander off to the sides. We walk about twenty yards, and they stop to graze.

Morning after morning, The Lambs and I walk to the front corner of the property. They glance around, not as though they're worrying about any threat, but just enjoying the cool, clean air as much as I am. Their long Karakul ears flop against their heads as they bounce along. Occasionally, one reaches down for a quick snip of grass. I notice that Chopin is deserting her sisters Mozart and Debussy to join the Charpentier-Satie formation, still the smallest ones in the group. Perhaps she has decided they need her protection. All I know is that now her wide black frame trudges along behind pure white Charpentier and Satie in his red polka-dot clown outfit.

All the younger lambs avoid the edge of the stream. The ewes

Sheep in parterre. (ABOVE LEFT) *The original flock of thirteen is now down to eleven sheep. Starting in the lower right corner, you can see Saint-Saëns, Ginastera, then Chopin's black face, and Debussy on the right. Mozart is directly behind Chopin (note that the ewes stay together). Charpentier stands beside Mozart, and Bach is behind her. Poulenc is behind Bach. On the right is Satie, with the beautiful red markings on his face. Then comes Ravel, and at the end is Couperin.*

Walking up the road to the forest. (BELOW LEFT) *I am not aware of any time when Ginastera gathered his troops to walk as far as the front pasture. But it was not uncommon for him to lead them up the road as far as the forest, as in this image. There was one amusing incident when I was out behind the house with several people, discussing the layout of a formal garden. Out of nowhere came Ginastera, leading his flock along the streambed below, as unconcernedly as though they performed this ritual every day.*

Chopin. *Chopin had short little bowlegs and did not glide around like Debussy and the glamorous Mozart. From the beginning, she assumed the task of protecting the smallest lambs, Satie and Charpentier. We nicknamed her the "nursemaid."*

ignore it. But Ginastera and Couperin find it irresistible. "A trait of sheep is that they never go near running water," the breeder had said. But this pair follows me through shoulder-high bulrushes to its brink. In most places, the stream lies on its back, softly floating through its thirty-foot-wide channel around the farm. Some stretches are crowded into narrow passages, shaded by enormous sycamores, which allow just enough sunlight to dart through top leaves to make the water sparkle.

The men tell various versions of when the stream overruns its banks. But by now, I have heard many stories about floods and bears and murders. It is inconceivable that the run that meanders around Le Berceau might do anything but ripple along the perimeter of the farm.

The border of the stream is uneven. In several places, erosion has carved out great hollows the size of respectable swimming pools. Elsewhere, the land leans into the water. One such place is my favorite. It's probably a little more than a hundred feet across, an almost perfect half circle of ground that extends out toward the water. Along its border are six old sycamores that are capped by leaves fifty feet above the ground. Because the stream narrows here, there is almost always the indeterminate music of lively water. This, with shade from the trees, is a perfect enclosure.

On daily walk around the streambed. As the fields were systematically cleaned of scrub trees and other debris—we found an old refrigerator deserted at the far end of the property—The Lambs and I were able to extend our morning walks to the back of the grounds. In the image, we are walking along the streambed toward the far fields. The breeder had told me that sheep never approach running water. This was mostly true. Here the line stays well away from the bank. There were a few times when Ginastera—and Couperin, surprisingly—followed me through the high grasses to the very edge of the stream.

At the Big Table. *The Big Table quickly became the center of many happy meals. It was on the daily route to the front pasture, and many mornings, while The Lambs grazed in the patch of orchardgrass beyond it, I had time to read about the history of the Karakul sheep. There were many lunches with friends, some of these continuing into improvised dinners. Note that all the foods that were not intended for The Lambs had to be arranged down the center of the table. We learned this lesson rather quickly one Sunday afternoon when Chopin helped herself to an enormous bowl of steamed broccoli, Poulenc devoured an entire basket of bread, and Saint-Saëns ate a visitor's Panama hat that had been left on a chair.*

When the contractor makes his next visit, I take him down to this spot. "Isn't this the most perfect place for outdoor meals?" I ask.

"Not necessarily. I agree it's a lovely area, but you ought to wait to see what happens in the next flood. You could find your lunch floating to Fredericksburg."

But the idea of dining under the sycamores is overpowering. Two of the carpenters cement table bases of our own fieldstones to the earth. Then they bolt steel tracks onto them to support a ten-foot-long tabletop.

The Big Table is the centerpiece of most visits. I make a long rose-garlanded tablecloth and begin gathering chairs to paint metallic gold. Tin plates with reproductions of Sèvres flower baskets, along with a collection of old silverware, and we have created a convincing backwoods nod to outdoor rooms at Versailles. The Lambs are always part of the scene. Ginastera dives under the table and comes out with the tablecloth caught on his little horns. Anyone in the way is tipped out of his chair.

Evening stroll. Toward the end of the day, I always walked down to the front gates to make sure that they were locked. During the day, especially if we were receiving guests, the gates remained open. The Lambs never ventured into the lane, nor did they make any attempt to enter the neighbor's wood, even though there was no fenced boundary. It was as though they were perfectly content with the contours of the environment that we walked every day and felt that no further exploration was really necessary.

27

First Snow

There is snow this winter. We haven't had any for several years, and The Lambs have never seen it. When it drifts into the security paddock, they eye it suspiciously. Finally, Ginastera and Bach venture out, their rear feet leaving a pattern of interwoven sled tracks. They make no effort to uncover grass. They bite off a few shoots that poke up through the snow and quickly retreat to the barn.

I would love to go for a walk in it with them, but I'm not disappointed that they decline. One might slip on the ice hidden between tufts of grass. Walks discontinued, I spend the mornings in the run-in. When they settle down to chew, I sit on the step.

Bach usually stands beside me until he decides to flop down at my feet, inviting me, it seems, to stroke the long straight fibers of his beige wool. Saint-Saëns's curlier fleece never leaves my side. Together, we look out at a huge cedar tree that collects the snow with steady serenity. Beyond it is a file of furry purple hickory trunks.

The first snow. We all sat in the run-in to watch the first snow that had fallen in Virginia for several years. The Lambs observed the phenomenon, but they did not seem eager to venture out in it. Very little snow accumulated, and after the sun was high, I thought they might be curious about walking in it. They moved along rather gingerly, stopping occasionally to nip a shoot of grass. When we stopped, they bunched tightly together. I took this as an indication that they would be happier in the barn.

Walking beside the forest in winter. Later that day, we took our usual walk down to the front pasture. Everyone was somewhat subdued. Ginastera chugged along, but there was no jumping for joy on this particular day. I would learn later that sheep are reluctant to walk where they are uncertain about their footing.

Across the road, tall pines that look like grizzled old men mark the edge of the forest.

By midday, the sun melts the inch or two of snow. We go out in the cold, clarifying air. It can never be too cool for sheep wrapped in fifteen pounds of wool.

Into the barn. The barn is a very compact structure, built into the slope. The Lambs are approaching the large front doors. The lower level was a storage area for tractors and what would become the Clubhouse apartment. The balcony of the loft bedroom is at the back of the building. This was one of my favorite spots. From this balcony, I could observe The Lambs in the paddock below and take in a long view of the entire field on that side of the property, including the meandering stream and the band of old maples and sycamores along its bank.

At the annual meeting of our firm, which is always held in New York to coincide with the lighting of the Christmas tree in Rockefeller Center, we officially terminate the business.

I will always miss the sheer theater of marching—in formation—into the corporate headquarters of our clients. Together, as a tight little unit and with immense resourcefulness and creativity, we have pioneered a field of law, and each of us has gained tremendous confidence by rising to the unexpected challenges of our clients.

In retrospect, it is clear that our timing could not have been better. My two Swiss corporate clients would enter mergers, which were more in the nature of takeovers, and in the process, many of the cultural programs we had established would be lost. The American representative of one of my favorite Japanese corporations would be promoted to a higher position and recalled to their Tokyo headquarters; another one would die suddenly. All of this occurred within two years after the closing of the firm. To reconstitute my client list would have been daunting.

Looking back, I would say that my soul had been watching out for me, although I did not understand that at the time.

The lambs greeting us. This is a fine display of The lambs with their beautiful full coats, although by now all dramatic black or copper fleeces have faded to beige or gray above their characteristically slender black Karakul legs. There are actually eleven sheep in this image, but Debussy is behind Bach and shows only her right ear; Satie is almost completely obscured by Ravel's magnificent presence; and only Poulenc's legs can be seen behind Mozart. You can see Charpentier is behind Couperin, nipping grass. From the left you have Bach, Saint-Saëns, Ginastera, Ravel, Chopin, Couperin, and Mozart.

28

Longer Morning Walks

Before long, there are fresh new leaves of the most delectable tender grass. Once again the countryside reaches out with renewed firmness of heart. The bitter silence of icy January gives way to a chorus of airborne voices as birds refresh their nests. Soon the redbud branches will be covered with clumps of tiny flowers, and buds on the dogwood trees at the edge of the dismal forest promise springtime.

The Lambs and I extend our daily walks. We begin at the front corner and follow the stream all around to the other side of the property.

As the days gradually warm, grazing in front of the Big Table can take more than an hour. Now that I have this table, I often carry with me whatever volume of Persian history I'm looking into. It is not an ideal setting for study, with Ginastera under the table scratching his back and Saint-Saëns gnawing the back of my chair. I see a lot of his mouth. While all the others have flesh-colored mouths, Saint-Saëns's is an entire cavity of licorice black—black tongue, black gums, and teeth that bite or nip any tempting page, chair, skirt hem, shoestring, or button.

Today I am brave enough to have brought a thermos of tea and a book. I have discovered a tale that is so engaging that I risk Saint-Saëns taking a bite of an antique page. I am reading _Travels in Central Asia_, by Armenius Vámbéry, a Hungarian Jewish scholar who made his trip in 1863 disguised as a Sufi dervish. Today, Saint-Saëns is generous and stays with his flock in the field. It is not out of courtesy to me. Fresh new sprouts of orchardgrass prevail over yellowed pages.

Into the front pasture from the pond. _In the front pasture, just below the bank of the pond, there is a wide expanse of orchardgrass. The Lambs could spread out and leisurely enjoy this delicacy for hours in the afternoon. With a bit of searching, they might even find some clover tucked down among the grasses. Often the sun would have gone on over behind the forest, and I could lie down here for a long siesta while The Lambs grazed._

The few clouds in the clear, wide sky are motionless. The front pasture is a swirl of green. It has an innocent glow, as though lit by the first dawn. Nothing can add to its pure and simple joyfulness. Water splashes over a log. A sharp herbal scent rises off wild grasses at the water's edge. Bark on trees, which I thought was uniformly brown, fades from taupe to lavender and sometimes disappears into battleship gray. Shapes between giant trees are sculpted into pitch-black constructions.

At the edge of the forest, an enormous old tulip-poplar presides over the entire front field. Although Pan, preeminent deity of the pasture and patron of pastoral poetry, is generally associated with the pine tree, this tree is a perfect monument to the half-human, half-goat god. We have to imagine that he carries his famous pipes. Pan was abundantly lustful and in constant hot pursuit of the nymphs, but he was also their faithful companion, accompanying their rounds with his music. Here he will protect The Lambs, who are searching out orchardgrass at his feet.

We are all clustered around the bench at the pond one morning when suddenly The Lambs freeze into sheep statues. Then, in a flash, they fly off in all different directions. I see a lost beagle loping across the front of the property. The poor dog, frightened by all the frenzy, zips up the lane. I had always thought that sheep instinctively herded together to repel attacks.

As soon as we're back in the barn, I telephone our county extension agent, who has years of experience with herd animals. Yes,

he explains, sometimes they will bunch together. But there is another innate defense behavior. He says, "If they can see the danger
right in front of them, there's a stimulus that informs them that a
predator can harm only one of them at a time. That's why they
scatter."

Several weeks later, as we are scoring our path around the bend of
the lower pasture, I recognize another reassuring pattern. One of
the three older males is always beside me—Bach or Saint-Saëns or
Ginastera. Only one, never all three of them, is either at my side or
immediately behind me, regardless of where I am in the group.
After a time, apparently according to some silent signal, they
change guard.

The sky is the color of bluebirds, several of which are darting
from one tree to the next. Suddenly, I stop. Here I am, out at the far
end of the property, alone with The Lambs. First I smile to myself.
But then I wonder whether this is wise. One neighbor says she
walks her dogs with a shotgun over her shoulder. What business do
I have enticing eleven young sheep out here where there isn't even a
fence?

They're not concerned, and I know by now that they are more
sensitive to danger than I am. Before I see the deer on the other side
of the stream, the designated watchers register its presence. Necks
stiffen; ears jut forward.

I know that I'm responsible for their safety, but I have never felt
more at ease, more secure, than I do today, with them. We continue

During morning stroll. *The Lambs are not nipping the grass here. They are indulging in one of their favorite pastimes: eating fresh dead leaves, what we referred to as "lamb potato chips."*

our lazy walk. Back inside their paddock by the barn, we arrange ourselves on the grassy slope to spend an hour together looking down onto the trees lining the stream.

So fulfilling and so complete is my time alone here that I feel as though my eyes have been fully opened and that for the first time in my life I see everything around me. I am totally exposed and available to the sounds and smells and textures surrounding me as nature draws me into the embrace of that special kind of solitude, what the ancients referred to as *otium*, studied leisure.

I have read that to truly develop self-knowledge, one must be solitary. Then, too, I am reminded of what has been said of the practice of centering prayer—that by quieting one's thoughts, one sheds meaningless things and habits and discovers one's truth. Whether it is because of the sumptuousness of everything around me or the direct effect of meditation, I can't help but marvel at how little I seem to need, of possessions, of people.

Now the hours that I choose to share are extremely precious. My preferred visit is with one carefully selected friend at a time, the ease to sit together under the old cedar tree with a bottle of wine, an apple. Or to pass an afternoon taking turns playing the old piano in the barn with The Lambs crowded around us.

29

Fortitude

Couperin is struggling to keep up with the group. My guess is that his heavy tail is the problem. My neighbor agrees. "That tail must weigh at least forty pounds. It must put awful pressure on his back." Even the pastoral nomads of the Karakuls' distant past, who depended upon the tails for fat, kept their sheep's tails shorter than Couperin's.

The old vet comes for an inconclusive examination. He wants to keep Couperin under observation at his clinic. My neighbor and I roll our eyes, but before noon we are clamping the cover onto the pickup bed. Couperin shows his mettle by standing during the entire thirty-minute ride along a winding county road. Doc ushers him into a large rear stall, where he will stay for two days. We visit him twice a day. He is standing, staring into a corner, seemingly unconcerned. My neighbor asks, "If the problem is that tail, couldn't he go somewhere to have it shortened?" I suppose this is a logical sugges-

Up to the pond in the front pasture. Here you can see Couperin at the far end of the group, making a heroic effort to keep up. You can also see how much longer his tail is than the others'. We always attributed his difficulties to the length—and therefore weight—of his tail.

Ravel. Ravel, another one of the younger lambs, stayed beside Couperin and was generally very agreeable. We will never forget, however, that once in the process of being shorn, he broke away from the shearer and went running across the security paddock with half his body cleanly shorn and the other side with a full coat of wool. We were so astonished by this sight that all we could do was stand and laugh. When he had satisfied himself that he was indeed a free spirit, he returned to the shearer for the rest of his haircut.

tion. But our only option is to take him to the large-animal hospital at Virginia Tech, which is at least four hours away.

Before I can reply, the neighbor adds, "Maybe we just ought to get him home."

Ravel, with the glistening maroonish brown fleece, seems to have missed Couperin. He becomes his constant buddy. As Couperin struggles to keep up with the group, Ravel stays beside him. But Couperin is determined. He lumbers up the slopes, his heavy tail dragging almost to his hooves. His ears swing from side to side as he drives himself forward, cumbrously lifting one foot and then another. I ask myself, How long do I let this go on? Couperin wants no sympathy. He jerks his head higher and wobbles over to Ravel.

Couperin. Whether it was due to the uncommon length of his tail or some other cause, it became obvious that Couperin was straining to move. We admired his determination and fortitude, but there were times that we found it difficult to watch. His friend Ravel stayed by his side, even when he did not feel like joining the others to graze in a favorite pasture.

30

Flood

Our spring rainy season begins gently enough, bringing the promise of healthy hay crops. Usually the rain that starts during the night stops by seven the next morning, in time for our morning stroll. But one day in late April, we make our entire circuit in a steady downpour that began around midnight. By the afternoon, it intensifies, falling diagonally. I sip tea from my perch on the end of a feed trough while The Lambs lie in the run-in, sniffing the cool air that rises off the wet earth.

The rain continues that night, lulling me into a deep sleep. I wake early the next morning, just before dawn. There is an odd sound. What is this roar? It sounds mechanical, like an auxiliary generator, which I do not have. With the early-morning light, an amazing sight glues me to a window. A solid sheet of water covers the lower pasture and is creeping up the slope. The run is indeed capable of exceeding its banks.

The Lambs! I pull on my rain gear and dash to the barn. They do not greet me at the feed troughs. They pace restlessly around the run-in. The churning water is over the lower line of fence and is approaching the barn. How far will it come? Emergency plans run through my mind. Should I move The Lambs into my house?

Headlights! My loyal neighbor! His pickup is high enough off the ground to travel the lane, although he says he has to leave immediately because he knows his bridge will wash out. He reassures me that my road is okay but that the Big Table is completely submerged. "Should we try to move The Lambs to higher ground?" I ask him.

"I don't think the water has ever come up as high as the barn," he says as the moving band of reddish gravy continues to rise. Logs and branches show how fast the floodwaters race. They sail by like parade floats whose brakes have failed. The Lambs do not relax with any morning chewing. While I cannot take my eyes away from the brown ocean below us, they resolutely look away from it.

Around eleven o'clock, the rain stops. The floodwater continues to rise as runoff from the mountains accumulates, but by midafternoon it slowly ebbs away, until I can see the flattened lower fence. By evening, the stream ripples along inside its banks as though nothing unusual has happened.

The next morning, The Lambs and I dodge pools of water to go down to see whether the Big Table has surfaced. Long rows of sand stretch diagonally across the fields. Water-soaked logs and one enormous uprooted tree litter the front pasture.

So much for my fantasy of a teahouse at the edge of the stream.

Our soil contains a lot of sand, and the floodwater quickly seeps into the ground. As soon as it is dry enough, we plant a line of five water-tolerant dawn redwoods along the front of the property. Inspired by the files of clipped yews in classic French gardens, they are a perfect wall. The trees will spread to twenty-five feet across and eventually grow over seventy feet tall. We are all present for the installation: my father, neighbors, the contractor and his landscape architect friend, the nursery crew, and eleven excited, curious lambs.

The contractor's friend proudly exhibits the antique tape measure he uses on important occasions. With three trees settled into place, the contractor and his friend pull the cherished tape taut to check the next interval. Saint-Saëns strikes. *Snip!* Two cherished tapes! "That thing!" bellows the landscape man.

Everyone laughs when I call back, "He's not a thing. He's my lamb!"

31

Bottomland Completely Cleared

My neighbor invites The Lambs and me to walk through the entire lower level of perfectly cleared fields. The truckloads of scrappy shrubberies have given way to a bottom pasture that now wraps all the way around the other side to a boulder-studded hillside that rises up to the high point of the land. We extend our morning circuit. At our destination—where Rameau and Fauré lie—we can look directly down onto our starting point in the front pasture.

My sheep dream flashes through my mind. The sheep come to me in the downward cycle. But they leave my level of the stage in a spiral operating upward. From this day on, I am aware that our daily walks carry us up, spiraling around from the bottomland to the graves.

Now that the ground-clearing project is finished and the barn is complete, there are very few interruptions. I am perfectly happy that no one is pounding on the office door to ask me a question. I often spend entire days with The Lambs. My neighbor was correct. Sheep really need very little actual care. But I love their company, and by choice they are my full-time occupation.

This is the perfect opportunity for me to seriously begin delving into the homeland of the Karakul sheep. This is a challenge. I do not even know where Central Asia is, and I am wondering if I will ever be able to sort out all the overlapping early peoples and cultures that have occupied this vast area.

On my next trip to Washington, I purchase an immense—seven feet by five feet—colored map of Central Asia. As soon as I return home that evening, I tack it to the back wall of the barn. It looks to me like a no-man's-land.

In the field across the road from the forest. (ABOVE LEFT) *Once all the fields were cleared, we made a complete circuit of the property every morning, starting in the front pasture, progressing around the far end of the lower pasture, and then gradually ascending to the high ground, seen here, across the road from the forest. Behind the cluster of sheep in the center of the image stands one of the tall old tulip-poplars, around which we would eventually wrap the canes of the climbing roses. Just out of sight to the left is the place we have designated as the pets' cemetery. Soon after this picture was taken, we began to mark the graves with oval white marble stones bearing the names of our departed.*
Peace on earth. (BELOW LEFT) *The Lambs all together beside the back terrace of the house, waiting for me to join them for an afternoon walk.*

Kazakhstan lies across the top one-third. In the upper left corner is the Aral Sea. From that point, Uzbekistan is a wide diagonal strip that runs down to the top of Afghanistan in the center of the map. To the west and parallel to it, there is another wide band, this one comprising Turkmenistan. I can see a tip of Iran in the lower left corner.

East of Uzbekistan there are thick horizontal layers of Kyrgyzstan and Tajikistan, both of which conclude in very high mountain ranges bordering Siberia, Mongolia, and China. The mountains are red and bronze on the map, like Ginastera. The vast inland expanses of deadly sands are more the color of Bach and Mozart.

I struggle to find someplace I recognize. At least I can locate the city of Bokhara. The former khanate of Bokhara is now roughly the territory that the republic of Uzbekistan occupies. (At one time, the area was referred to as Turkistan; in older references, it is Transoxiana.) The Pamir Mountains form its southern boundary. To the east and north, the steppes run out to surrounding forest walls.

Its western boundary, the ancient Oxus River (now renamed the Amu Darya) flows eighteen hundred miles from the heights of the Pamirs to the Aral Sea. The Oxus is remembered as one of the medieval rivers of paradise. On the banks of this hallowed waterway and its tributaries rose the noble cities of antiquity. Their names echo with distant memories of Alexander the Great and the Mongol warlord Genghis Khan: Bokhara, Samarkand, Balkh, Khiva.

The tiny village of Karakul is about fifty miles from Bokhara, in the valley of the Amu Darya. This poor sand-swept village provides the name for my breed. Legend has it that the famous tight curls on the pelts of lambs born here are due to a diet of wild wheat. The mountainous deserts—with elevations up to eight thousand feet—sparse food supplies, long distances to water, and a generally hard life produced the extremely hardy Karakuls.

As much as I want to learn about the origins of The Lambs, I foresee that Central Asia will be an elusive study. Through the centuries, boundaries in this sprawling landmass of deserts, mountains, and steppes have shifted with each wave of invaders. As recently as the turn of the nineteenth century, there were areas that had never been mapped. Some of them were not claimed by any country because Central Asia was dismissed as a peripheral zone, the backyard of one of the great powers. Only recently—in the process of creating the republics of Uzbekistan, Turkmenistan, Kazakhstan, Tajikistan, and Kyrgyzstan—was it clearly defined.

32

Festival

The breeder telephones to suggest that I attend the Maryland Sheep and Wool Festival, where he will be showing his Karakuls. I know how much my lambs have captivated me, but until this event, I did not appreciate the fascination with sheep. People who don't own sheep or even work with wool travel for miles to watch parades of different breeds and spinning demonstrations. What is it about sheep? What is it that draws us to them?

Perhaps it is the typical visual image of a flock of sheep with its shepherd, the shepherd apparently present for no other reason than to look after his animals. Is it that we are hungry to receive such care ourselves? Perhaps this explains why a carefully maintained garden— or friendship—affects us with such force.

That sheep are animals requiring careful tending is revealed in their distinct vernacular species name, according to Richard Lydekker. The word *sheep* is of ancient Sanskrit derivation (suggesting

Eastern ancestry), and is the equivalent of the Anglo-Saxon *sceap*, the Danish *schaap*, the German *schaf*, the Latin *ovis*, and the Greek *oïs*, all derived from the Sanskrit *avi*, which is a modification of the root *av*, which means "to keep" or "to guard."

To the ancient Egyptians, the sheep was a god. They had appropriated Ammon—a god in the shape of a ram—from the Libyan desert tribesmen. They believed that their version of the god, Amun of Siwa, lord of good counsel, transmitted the potency of the ram's masculine strength into their human world, along with his innate ability to control his power and abide peaceably in his flock.

As sacred beings, rams were never killed in the regular ritual practices. However, at the god's annual festival, one ram was sacrificed. The officiating priest then dressed in the animal's skin, in the belief that he was taking the spiritual essence of the ram into himself and could then, in turn, impart it to his people.

During the day at this festival, I not only witness the interest in sheep but come to appreciate my own distinction as a guardian of rare Karakul sheep. Standing beside the penned Karakuls, I overhear the woman next to me gushing to her friend over their color variations. At one point, she turns to inform me, "These are the sheep that produce Persian Lamb. I absolutely have to have some of their wool for my first spinning project."

For some reason, I can't resist telling her that my Karakuls are even more colorful. I am not too surprised that the very next day she drives down from northern Virginia to see The Lambs. She is thrilled

Bach loves Chartreuse. We placed another old green bench under a massive tree at the far end of the security paddock. It seemed like a good idea to keep a tin cup and a bottle of Chartreuse, which a guest brought, under this bench. One chilly day, my father opened the bottle. Bach came swiftly and took a long gulp from the cup. We discussed this at length over dinner that evening and concluded that since Chartreuse contains fermented herbs, Bach thought this was liquid hay. No one else was interested, but the two of them got through enough of it that we periodically replaced the bottle.

with them. And she tells me so many details about her new spinning wheel that I begin to wonder if she'll ever leave. I think she is
going to faint with pleasure when I show her the bag of Rameau's
lustrous black fleece, but I offer it to her to get rid of her. When she
telephones to thank me later that evening, she asks if she can make
something for us.

Well, how about a hat? It would be a nice souvenir of Rameau to
give to my father. The summer months go by, and I forget about the
project. Then one day, her highly original piece arrives in the mail.
It looks more like a product of felting than of spinning, and it is
much too heavy to be worn, but it will always remind us of Rameau
and is therefore a treasure. I put it away for my father.

He will be ninety years old in November, and we organize a dazzling birthday party during his autumn visit. While he and I are
walking through the lower pasture one morning, I tell him I have
a very unusual present for him. His face lights up with his typical
pleasure at the slightest thing. Then he tells me, "Say, darling, you
know how I've always wanted to study ancient Greek? Well, I've
decided to sign up for the beginning course at Carroll College next
semester."

This is important news, and it makes me happy that he is still
taking on new challenges. But I notice that his pace is slower than
ever and that we are barely moving as we progress through the field.
I can't help asking myself if I am selfish to encourage him to travel
all the way to Le Berceau. I know how much he enjoys being here,
the company of The Lambs and me, and the freedom to do whatever
he wants. But I also know that the traveling is arduous and that it
takes effort to be a good guest, even when one feels completely

wanted. Some mornings, there are dark circles under his eyes. Occasionally, he has a new, slightly hollow look, which pierces me. It suggests to me a distance, even absence.

When his pace first began to slacken, I found it difficult to slow my own. Now, after moving for months at the speed of The Lambs, we all easily amble along together. His hearing has greatly deteriorated. Repeating myself is tedious, but whenever I find myself in need of patience, I ask myself, Do you think he really wanted to go to all those childhood piano recitals?

The excitement of being here is costing him some rest. I know he retires in the afternoons in Montana, and I will have to think of some way to trick him into afternoon naps. There is a lovely platform of ground about two feet above the water at the back of the property—the perfect place for a siesta.

All of these concerns are with me when I enter my house. And what do I find? Mozart's *Requiem* at the loudest-possible volume. My father, seated in the small sitting room, his eyes closed, with the shimmer of such ecstasy on his face that I resolve to do whatever I can to continue his visits for as long as he wants.

33

Drought

The seasons pass. Winter, spring. We perform our daily rituals, the walks around the perimeter of the farm, centering prayer, meals at the Big Table. Summer comes early. At the Farmers Co-op, there is talk of a serious drought. Having seen all that floodwater, I dismiss the idea until suddenly the grass is crackling under my feet, and there is not so much as a trickle of water in the stream. Tiny patches of grass peek out of the sediment at the bottom. I telephone my father.

"Oh, honey, don't worry. It will come back as quickly as it dried up."

The next morning, Satie is coughing. I would dismiss it because there is so much dust in the air, but he coughs incessantly. The old vet is away at a conference. But our county extension agent says a promising new vet has just arrived in the area. An hour later, young Dr. Patrick Comyn, in a crisp plaid cotton shirt and khaki pants, bounces into the barn. I blink in delighted disbelief. Satie has pneu-monia, he concludes, and a dangerously high temperature. "It's un-likely he'll pull through in this weather," he says. "It's contagious, you know. We can't take any chances with the others." By the time my neighbor arrives, Satie rests in peace. The men gently lift Satie's body into the pickup bed. Wrapped in an old flowered bedspread, he will travel to a local funeral home, which has begun a practice of cremating pet animals.

Dr. Comyn has no idea how valuable his youthful vigor, sturdy form, and clear eyes are to me. His years of specialized training in ruminant animals at the distinguished veterinary school of Montana State University were entirely focused on cattle. "You will be my graduate school!" he proclaims. "These guys are really unusual. Five-year-old sheep are rare. By this time, they've usually been eaten either by wolf or by man."

He comes often to check for pneumonia. The combination of dust, heat, and humidity taxes the delicate lungs of sheep. With his guidance, we upgrade our strategies for hot weather protection. "What you really need," he announces, "is a proper set of window fans." He locates a fan manufacturer in South Carolina, and before the end of the month, he is directing the installation of two blue cone-shaped fans so that they pour misty air into the center of the barn. The Lambs run to the far walls. "They'll come to terms with them," Dr. Comyn assures me, and within minutes, Ginastera is turning his back into the mist from one of them, as though he is under a shower. Bach claims the best position in front of the other one. Saint-Saëns paces around in front of Ginastera, not quite sure about this phenomenon. For the others, the fans will have to wait.

I miss Satie. He was detached, but his brilliant terra-cotta dots were so festive, so theatrical. Chopin clings steadfastly to Charpentier. I notice that on our morning walks, The Lambs move in a tighter formation. It seems that they are closing in to protect one another. According to Konrad Lorenz, no predator charges into a tight group of prey animals, no matter how defenseless they may be. If it is true that there is safety in numbers, then surely The Lambs feel more vulnerable than ever before.

How do I relate Satie's death to my father? Do I telephone? Do I write? I remember that when he had a heart attack a few years ago, he waited until he could deliver the news to me in person. I follow that example, uncomfortably, until he arrives for a long Thanksgiving holiday. It is so good to see him again and to sense his delight to be back at Le Berceau. Now, here he is, full of anticipation of being at the farm and spending time with his special friend, Satie, news of whom I have withheld. Whom was I protecting? Him? Myself? Would it have been more honest to tell him by telephone and let him absorb the news by himself? Or was the better choice to be with him when I delivered it? Either way, love was involved, and there will be a price.

"Well, I'd like to go down to the barn to see my friend Satie," he says as soon as he finishes his drink.

"Daddy, there is something I have to tell you."

He focuses his thoughtful eyes on me.

"Daddy, I remember how you insisted on waiting until we were together to tell me about your heart attack."

"Is something wrong with Satie, honey?"

Debussy. Debussy was extremely sensitive. There was one time when I felt particularly sad after my father had departed to return to his home in Montana. As far as I knew, I was not exhibiting my feelings in any way, but from that moment on, Debussy attached herself to me by placing her chin in the palm of my left hand. We made our morning circuit as a unit, Debussy and I.

"Daddy . . ." I say, and give him a summary of the sad news.

I am watching him closely for a reaction. He does not so much as blink. Then he looks down and sits absolutely still. I know it is impossible to understand the depth of anyone's feeling for another creature, and I can only imagine that he is rearranging his mind to accept the loss of Satie, who was such a faithful and adoring companion when he was here with us.

After what seems like ten minutes, I reach over to place my hand on his arm. He looks at me with his clear blue eyes and says, "Well, if you don't mind, I think I'll call it a day."

I accompany him down to his quarters in the barn. He is quiet as we approach the door. How will it feel to see The Lambs moving around without the red polka-dot costume among them? And what will he be thinking when he takes them for their morning stroll? "Don't worry, honey. I know you did what you thought was right," he says.

There are other concerns. I watch the effort he makes to rise from a chair. Sometimes I stand just out of his view and watch him as, it seems, he commands his limbs to organize themselves into an upright position. The weather doesn't help. Day after day, the sky is gray and the air is thick with fog. I will throw away all the grainy photographs of this visit. Even a chicken cooked according to Henri IV's all-day method fails to lift spirits.

This time—and for the first time ever—when he leaves, I feel empty. Desolate. What would life here be without the expectation of his irrepressible energy and joy and gratitude for every tiny thing?

My heart is heavy when I take The Lambs out for our walk the next morning. I am in the center of the group with the ewes. We are passing a wide section of the stream when I feel something in my left hand. I look down. Debussy's chin! Does she sense how alone I feel? From that moment on, every time we make our circuit, she and I stroll together as a unit. The soft apricot curls that part on her head are comforting to me. She rarely lifts her eyes as she faithfully plods along beside me.

Charpentier. I was always surprised by the rare beauty of Charpentier, so pure white and so exquisitely formed. His spirit, too, was lovely. But he was also intelligent, and from time to time, he attempted to lead the group. He succeeded on one occasion. There must have been some earlier consultation among them. I watched from an upstairs balcony as Charpentier—with the others directly behind him—approached the fence that was protecting the ten miniature boxwoods that were arranged in the parterre behind the house. The Lambs had always been bothered by that low wire fencing. Charpentier raised one foot and smashed the fence. The Lambs rushed in, each one heading directly toward what appeared to be an assigned plant. This performance happened so quickly that I knew all of the boxwoods would be eaten down to the ground before I could run downstairs to intervene. It was preferable simply to enjoy the spectacle.

34

Losing Your Wingman

The next year is uneventful until we reach the end of June. With no warning, I find Ravel lying on the ground, obviously in agony. Dr. Comyn arrives. Ravel is suffering from a blockage of the urinary tract. There is no relief to offer. We perform our sad ritual. But for his loyalty to Couperin, Ravel was an obscure presence among the younger lambs. And yet, his death registers, and I am left with a primitive feeling of debt for the snuffing out of a life.

Couperin has lost his only faithful buddy. "In every group of herd animals," Dr. Comyn tells me, "each one has a wingman. That's the problem when the group gets smaller. They lose their wingman." Perhaps I only imagine that Couperin weakens. But I think his effort to walk intensifies. Each movement seems more labored. His face sags; he seems mildly bewildered.

Then comes the day when I am preparing for weekend guests. I return from town with a load of flowers. Just as I emerge from my car, I see Couperin awkwardly approaching me. He loses his footing. He collapses. It happens so quickly. From where I stand, it looks like he falls on his neck. I race to summon my neighbor.

We run to rescue the poor broken heap. In the barn, he solidifies into a standing position. I reach Dr. Comyn at a nearby farm. There are no choices. Couperin has outlasted his handicap longer than anyone would have guessed. There is the usual coming together. Dr. Comyn injects the deep-sleep medication.

Couperin breathes heavily. His body stiffens, and he falls. Not by folding or sliding along Dr. Comyn's leg, but like a solid wood statue toppling over. Perhaps his muscles have memorized this posture in the years of willing himself to stay upright. He lies on the ground in precisely the position he held while standing. It is as if he is announcing to us, I have known a good life. And with that, all of my younger lambs, except for fat Poulenc and pure white Charpentier, are gone.

35

Buried Treasure

This year, by mid-August, seventeen tropical storms are gathering over the Atlantic Ocean. One by one, they collapse or move into the Caribbean. All but one. By the first week of September, Hurricane Isabel is approaching southern Virginia.

I collect gallons of bottled water, since the well is electrified and stops working if the power goes off. Isabel continues toward us. I reluctantly purchase tins of vegetables, a jar of peanut butter, and a carton of saltines. Isabel is indeed coming into Virginia. She will pass directly over us. I wisely shampoo my hair. Two neighbors rush around to gather the bench at the pond and the gold chairs. Later in the afternoon, they go back out to unbolt the heavy pine tabletop to store in the barn. A quiet golden September day concludes as a gentle wind comes up.

The Lambs and I sit in the run-in as darkness approaches and the wind strengthens. The roof of the barn screams with each lash of the

105-mile-per-hour wind. I turn the light switch. Electricity is gone. I stay with The Lambs. They range against the run-in wall, looking out into the storm. They are interested, but not restless as they were during the flood. No one sleeps.

In the early dawn, I watch the wind catch the tip of a young dogwood and fold it to the ground. With daylight comes a pause in the wind. The Lambs shuffle over to the feed troughs for their morning Prime Lamb. I fill buckets with bottled water. When my neighbor comes to see if we have survived, we go out to survey the damage. But for a few small trees lying across the road, we have escaped.

However, our rural electricity company announces that we will be without power for a while. At least The Lambs and I can resume our morning and evening walks. I gather limbs snapped off during the storm. I sip cool champagne with peanut butter and saltines. I rinse dishes with Listerine. One-minute baths become routine, and the offer of a trip to the village motel for a shower seems unsporting. I pass the days playing the old piano and reading Philip Glazebrook's *Journey to Khiva*, which brings a sense of proportion to my inconveniences. But during this time, our lives change forever when I make a chance discovery.

As the week without power drags on, I search my reserves for interesting things to eat. Nothing. Then, in the loft, in a decorative tin that doubles as a bedside table, I find a brown paper bag of Murray's gingersnaps. I rip open a corner as I descend the stairs. Potent spices blast through the barn. Bach, Ginastera, and Saint-Saëns come running. At their heels are Chopin and Mozart and Debussy. Poulenc and Charpentier follow. Gingersnaps disappear in seconds.

Dr. Comyn says The Lambs probably recognize the molasses of

their Prime Lamb. "Just don't let them have too many of those things," he advises. Forget it! We are so completely distracted by gingersnaps that we are (I am) almost disappointed when the power returns. Back to sensible diets and reasonable bedtimes.

It is autumn. The temperature drops. The days shorten. Ginastera jumps into the air as we glide down freshly mowed slopes. He runs; others follow, tails flying. We have lived through a drought and three deaths and a hurricane. There is music everywhere. And gingersnaps!

Man with gingersnaps in his pocket. *To have a hurricane pass over our heads was dramatic, but it did not produce the lasting effects of the discovery of an old bag of Murray's gingersnaps. You can see one of the paper bags of these remarkable treats in the barn window. We were famous for them. We gave them as souvenirs of visits; guests brought them as hostess presents; one guest contributed a pie with a gingersnap crust to a dinner here. Even Dr. Comyn conceded that there could never be too many gingersnaps.*

36

Eight Lambs

Run, Ginastera, run, with your sizzling orange tail flopping on your rump—*whop, whop, whop*—who cares that you aren't supposed to run, that you strain your lungs, your knees, your legs? Run, run for no good reason, for the joy of being alive, no predator in pursuit. That's it, swing that massive red head left, then right. Front feet land together; back feet land together. Front, back, pound, pound, pound that pretty grass on the hill slope. You have nothing to do today but clatter down the hillside like a great rocking horse, front feet together, back feet together, tail—*whomp, whomp, whomp.*

You, too, Saint-Saëns? Well, why not? Ginastera springs off the ground. Swings around in the air. Thumps to the ground. Pound, pound, pound the grass into the earth. Saint-Saëns leaps, then runs behind his twin. Agile as Nijinsky. Now red legs, now black legs. Rhythm: Two front legs land together. Beat. Two back legs, two front legs. Beat. Beat. Two back legs. Hold. Throw a glance at the huge old cedar tree. This is the life.

Here comes Bach, bold as Ginastera but a master of old-world reserve. One solid sheath of silvered ivory. Sailing through the air, never touching the earth. Head up, focus straight. No jumping. Far too dignified for hurtling off the ground and landing, *thump*. But galloping? You bet. Nothing stops his loose-limbed panache.

Now gentle Debussy, always delicately stepping with her head in my hand, morning after morning, around the path by the stream. Run, little Debussy, white tail against white bottom—*whap, whap, whap*. Tail straight out behind in the air. All thirty pounds of tail in line with your back. Run, Debussy, run. Run to Ginastera. Off to the edge of the stream by the silver maple. White tail whipping up in the air and flopping onto your white bottom, flashing its fleshy pretty pink underside.

That's it, Saint-Saëns. Run past Ginastera. Skid to a stop in front of the tallest sugar maple. Chopin, you've never hurried in your life. Can your little bowlegged frame run? Go on, then, catch up with Debussy. Mozart flings her two hundred pounds into the air. Can you believe it? I never thought I'd see Mozart toss aside her Marlene Dietrich mask and race down a hill. *Ka-boom, ka-boom*. Front feet together, back feet together, right behind Chopin. At her heels, fat Poulenc.

He slides down the hillside to the edge of the stream. Whoa. Not easy to bring this body to a stop. But look at all the leaves on the ground. Sheep potato chips! Well, what are you waiting for, Charpentier? You aren't shy. Oh, but you're quick. In a flash, down with the others.

Isn't anybody thirsty? You know you aren't supposed to run like that. That's exactly how many a dog has killed a sheep. Sheer exhaustion from the chase. Ginastera, did you hear that? You always seem to be in the lead. Don't you feel responsible for them? No? Not on a day like this! Jump for joy!

37

The Forest

The next day, the early-morning light languidly rises beyond the forest. Pale pastels outline the treetops. At half past six, I go down to the barn. Mozart is sleeping with her head on Bach's back. Amazing. She is capable of physical contact. Ginastera patrols the security paddock. Only Poulenc is at a feed trough.

Saint-Saëns intercepts me between the bifolding doors with a friendly head butt against my knees. He wants a little scratching on the top of his head. Now he swerves to present his long, shapely back to me. This is an unspeakable pleasure, as his is the only double-layered fleece in the group. Under the carpet and saddle blanket guard hairs is a hidden layer of down. Well, Saint-Saëns, we'll continue this later. Now let's feed everybody and get ready for our big day.

My neighbor and a helper arrive early. "What are you doing here at this hour?" I ask.

"Well, we just couldn't wait."

For over a year, a day or two at a time, my neighbor, two helpers, and a giant wood-chipping machine have miraculously turned a scene of portentous gloom into one of natural glorification. And today we will take The Lambs through the section of the forest that is completely cleared.

Sheep are known to be excellent pathfinders. Their ancestors navigated around the glaciers of the early Ice Age. Surely they have some residual capacity to mark out a footpath in a contained little wood. I stuff a handful of blue surveyor's flags into my jacket pocket. "Let's go, lambs. A conquest!"

Ginastera bounds up the road. Bach lifts up into his striking noble grandeur. Debussy presses against my left leg, urging me to walk faster. Poulenc, digesting his double breakfast, passes Chopin, who plows forward like an armored tank.

The Lambs and I enter the upper level of the wood, carving a broad turn toward a promontory that overlooks the stream. To our right is the unexplored density of the forest. I stand back. The Lambs advance into a stand of huge hickories. Without hesitating, Ginastera moves to the front. No one interferes.

Next comes Bach. Then Saint-Saëns. Debussy, who habitually holds fast to my side, lands a head butt in Poulenc's considerable haunch and falls in behind Saint-Saëns. Poulenc follows Debussy, but Mozart shoves him away. Beauty before bulk. Will Poulenc hold his own against Chopin, who is chugging into place behind Mozart? Poor Poulenc. Shunned by the big boys and shooed away by the girls. He and Charpentier will negotiate the rearmost position.

No trail suggests itself through the masses of tall dark brown, black, mocha-lavender tree trunks. But The Lambs know exactly what to do: Eat! One head turns in one direction, the next in another. Slow progress into unknown territory with not the slightest worry. Down a shallow incline, past massive mossy boulders on the left, they thread their way through the trees until they traverse the lower section of the wood. Everyone gaily snatches freshly fallen leaves.

My job is to follow the line and plant the blue flags. Saint-Saëns considers the relative attraction of leaves and plastic flags. Reasoning that leaves are everywhere and flags rare, he bites the flags. Chopin joins him. I plant flags. Saint-Saëns and Chopin yank them up. I have time to replace enough flags to roughly mark the track.

Progress is slow, but we have our momentum. I can see where they're going. In an hour's time, we gently drop down parallel to the lower line of trees. Directly across the field from the Big Table, we make a full curve to sneak out of the wood as furtively as we entered above.

For the next two weeks, The Lambs solidify their oscillating path before pushing farther into the remote recesses of the wood. We have waited six years to penetrate these shadowy depths, and there is no cause to rush. From the opening that gives onto the field across from the Big Table—where the long tablecloth and gold chairs promise an outdoor Thanksgiving luncheon—The Lambs stretch out their line for the steep climb to the high ground. Chopin explores the fringe of trees at the border of the front pasture. She

On the path through the forest. As soon as the men had gathered the brambles and fallen trees from the floor of the wood and had pulled yards of poison ivy from high limbs, The Lambs were given the task of defining a network of paths through the dense old-growth forest. They accomplished this with great enthusiasm and skill. The lower path across the length of the forest is gently undulating. To connect this long stretch to the upper transverse path, Chopin and Debussy led the way in tracing a trail that wove around great piles of boulders, summoning us deeper into the density of the trees and conferring on every trip a sense of mystery and discovery. Several years later, we edged the paths with narrow logs held in place by pine stakes.

advances around another massive granite pile into a vast habitat of prickly cocklebur bushes. Debussy follows. The forest enchants the ewes. They have never before exhibited curiosity.

⁂

As soon as my father arrives for the Thanksgiving holiday, I hand him a glass of wine. I feel I owe him a spectacular visit. The forest will not disappoint. The Lambs lead him down their arboreous path.

"Well, honey, what's my assignment? What can I contribute to this work of art?"

"See that big granite boulder down there? I was hoping you'd figure out a way to make a little place to sit there. Can't you picture yourself leaning against the rock, reading poetry?"

A temple to poetry! The next day, he asks my neighbor to haul two railroad-tie segments to the moss-mottled rocks. In the village, we order a thin brass plate inscribed with a fragment of "Lines Composed a Few Miles Above Tintern Abbey" ("hardly hedge-rows, little lines / Of sportive wood run wild; . . .") to christen our poetry bench. He fills an old French candy tin with some of his favorite verse: Petrarch's Sonnet 307; "Reverie of a Business Man," by Horace; "Archaic Torso of Apollo," by Rilke; Walter de la Mare's "Fare Well"; and, of course, Wordsworth's "Intimations of Immortality from Recollections of Early Childhood." They will wait for him on the bench.

He is brave enough to sit there with The Lambs crowding all around for whatever lunch he optimistically carries in his knapsack. Saint-Saëns and Ginastera are merciless. They steal every morsel.

Poulenc is not shy about snatching the hat off his head. One after‑
noon, I arrive and find all of them breathing down on him. My poor
father is laughing as he waves both arms to fend off large eager sheep
faces. This little bench will remind us that poetry country is not
some place disconnected from daily life. Poetry may suffuse all of
our lives here, but there are times when we must address purely
practical concerns, such as fighting to defend our lunches.

The poetry bench in the forest. (ABOVE LEFT) It was my father's joy to establish
a "temple to poetry" in front of a great moss-covered rock on the lower path.
The poetry bench—two railroad-tie chunks secured with steel rods—became a
popular meeting place. He found an old French candy box to hold pages of his
favorite poems. We had a line from Wordsworth's "Lines Composed a Few Miles
Above Tintern Abbey" engraved on a brass strip to identify this construction.
There was often a bottle of good red wine stored behind the poetry bench.
At the poetry bench in the forest. (BELOW LEFT) The Lambs and my father
spent entire afternoons at the poetry bench. I was never too convinced that
much poetry reading was taking place, because whenever I arrived at the
scene, I witnessed large sheep clamoring for whatever lunch my father might
have carried down there in an old cotton knapsack. If you look carefully at
the moss on top of the rocks, you will see some of the blue plastic flags that
we used in laying out the paths. These flags may actually be the only ones
that Saint-Saëns and Chopin did not eat in the process.

38

Persian Heritage

The next morning, we settle in with the history of the Karakuls' birthplace. I've been hearing about the Medes and the Persians since I was a child, and I can see that my father can hardly wait. Like devoted coconspirators, we begin to thread our way into a remote corner of the fabled Persian Empire. Soon we will be accompanying caravans of sand-tolerant, double-eyelidded Bactrian camels along the old trading routes.

Alexander the Great is our breakfast topic. By crossing into Asia Minor in 334 B.C., he was continuing the work of his father, Philip of Macedonia. It is unknown precisely why he burned Persepolis, King Darius's symbol of magnificent kingship. But even that drama was not enough for Alexander. He plunged all the way across Persia to the far northeastern kingdom of Sogdiana, where the ancestors of The Lambs once grazed.

At that time, Samarkand was already a rich metropolis, fortified with eight miles of ramps and iron gates. The Sogdians were sophisticated people. Unlike their warrior neighbors, they were scholars and deal makers. From the age of five, Sogdian boys were primed to trade. They learned Arabic, Chinese, Turkic, and Tibetan, and as soon as they were old enough to leave home, they went out to sell the skins of newborn Karakul lambs to shahs and emirs. The Sogdians would be the undisputed masters of the trade routes (later known as the Silk Road) for seven hundred years.

It is a thrill to find the home of The Lambs in one of the world's oldest and most complex civilizations. Dreams of love and gardens, religious mysticism, splendid palaces and mosques, discoveries in mathematics, astronomy, and medicine. Resilient in crisis after crisis, bending to their conquerors but eventually gaining cultural leverage over them, the Persians ensured the survival of their language and intellectual heritage.

My father contributes his old volume of Herodotus to the loft library. Writing in the fifth century B.C., the Father of History describes how spices are gathered in Arabia. Then he writes, "I have said enough of the spices of Arabia; airs wondrous sweet blow from that land. They have moreover two marvelous kinds of sheep, nowhere else found. One of these has tails no less than three cubits long. Were the sheep to trail these after them, they would suffer hurt by the rubbing of the tails on the ground; but as it is every shepherd there knows enough of carpentry to make little carts which they fix under the tails, binding the tail of each several sheep on its own cart. *The other kind of sheep has a tail a full cubit broad* [my italics]."

This is a glorious visit. Persia. The poetry bench. This afternoon when I join my father there—he is encamped with a bottle of wine and a packet of Fig Newtons—he carefully unfolds a page of verse from the tin. Already the moisture has stained the edges of the paper with rust to match the box. He deliberates between Horace and Rilke before settling on "Archaic Torso of Apollo," which he reads to me. I am never prepared for the force of that last line: "You must change your life."

Then he asks me, "Do you remember that black leather-bound journal I purchased on our last trip to New York? I've started writing in it. I'm copying my favorite poetry into it. It is, of course, for you one day."

39

A Merry Christmas

As December deepens, the sky turns fluorescent silver behind the tree skeletons along the streambed. The air holds the moisture that promises snow, but none arrives. The Lambs cannot be happier. No heat, no flies, big barn doors open. They are never inside the barn during the day, and they happily join any activity. If I want to make a quick trip to the front of the property without them, I have to crawl on my hands and knees through the lower pasture. Even then I do not necessarily escape the watchful eyes of Saint-Saëns.

It is time to gather cedar branches for the medieval mantel in the music room. This is an involved undertaking because I have so much help. The warmhearted old cedar tree straddles the slope between the lower pasture and the high ground of the cemetery. It opens its arms wide as Bach and Poulenc tug on low boughs. Saint-Saëns and Mozart rise to nibble the needles that reach out over the bottom pasture. I snip branches and place them in my basket. Ginastera plunges in after them. He catches his horn nubs on the wicker handle and wildly tosses his basket face around until I notice. He loves this routine.

When my father arrives for Christmas, we crowd into my neighbor's pickup to visit the local tree farm. The next day, two friends drive down from Washington to help us install a magnificent twenty-foot-tall white pine. A huge fire blazes in the hearth. Plainchant clarifies the air. While the men secure the tree to upstairs balusters, my friends and I tie copper-painted twigs to the branches with wide metallic gold ribbons. All this time, The Lambs press their noses against the doors.

The Saturday before Christmas, we lay out a feast in the music room. There is a giant Virginia ham in rich mustard-lined bread crust, great pots of corn pudding, smoked salmon, brussels sprouts, special breads. The cauldron of wassail fills the room with the scent of ginger and cloves. My father, in bright red waistcoat and tartan trousers, stands at the door to greet old friends, who arrive with bags of presents, poetry to read by the fire, armloads of piano music.

Guests take their drinks outside to compare our terrain to that of their farms in France. Some settle in front of the fire to read poetry to one another. In the sitting room, several others decorate Christmas cookies (we will find tiny silver cake decorations in corners for months). As soon as one guest launches into Greek music on the piano, his wife starts to dance in the center of the room.

It is altogether too much for The Lambs. They push one another against the doors until somebody opens one. Ginastera heads for the piano. He yanks on the player's coattail while Saint-Saëns and Chopin proceed to the Christmas cookie operation. Mozart and Bach are dangerously interested in the tree. No one approaches the fire.

Cameras flash. There are only eight lambs, but dispersed around the house, they are everywhere. Poulenc eyes a great basket of breads, but someone whisks it away before he decides what to grab. Saint-Saëns cavorts around with a gold paper crown rakishly over one eye.

Lambs come in one door, go out another. Guests move from room to room, drinks in hand, ribbons around their necks. The Lambs gather around the piano for Christmas carols as day sinks into evening. No one wants to leave. Reluctantly, I escort The Lambs to the barn while guests pack up their bags of gifts and books.

The cheer of this day will easily carry us through the holidays and then through the January ice storms. It will take weeks to return all the scarves and eyeglasses and books that were forgotten in the spicy haze of that afternoon.

40

Joshua Arrives

Dr. Comyn tells me that one of his assistants is planning to make a living raising large animals and wants some experience working around sheep. He enthusiastically recommends this "kid" who already has his own twenty-five Jersey cows and has recently won the top herdsman and top showman awards at the state fair. "He's Mennonite," Dr. Comyn adds, "and, you know, they work all the time." I could certainly use some regular help maintaining the barn.

"Sure, I can do it! Just tell me what you want and when you want it!" And with that, seventeen-year-old Joshua Clemons springs into action. Skinny and six feet tall, he looks like he's made of wire, and he works like some sort of windup mechanism. He grabs the scoop shovel and races up and down the floor until his pickup bed is full of old sawdust. A few seconds later, he is in the lower pasture, flinging it around. Blink your eyes and there is a new thick bed of resin-rich sawdust on the floor.

"Won't you please take a break?" I beg. He does not comprehend. "At least drink some water."

"Like I told you, ma'am, I'm fine."

He does a lot more than help Dr. Comyn. Besides excelling in school and studying the violin, he has a full-time job as comanager of a herd of cows at a large local dairy farm. To fit me into the schedule, he arrives earlier and earlier in the mornings. There is the constant matter of his key to my gates.

Sheep at front door. Ginastera, who still has the tight copper red Karakul curls along the sides of his face, is in his morning position to lead his little flock out for their morning stroll around the streambed. Ginastera took up his position at the door at half past eight every single morning. The others would quickly fall into formation, although occasionally they had to wait until Poulenc had sucked up any stray grain pellets that were left in the feed troughs. You can see here the thick bed of pine sawdust that Joshua regularly maintained on the floor of the main room of the barn.

In addition to maintaining the barn, Joshua serenades moonlit dinners.
When Joshua arrived to help with the barn maintenance, it was like a lightning strike. He could sweep out the barn and add fresh sawdust before we could greet him. Bach immediately adopted him as his role model and faithfully followed him wherever he went. Joshua complained that he could not even go into the barn office to make a telephone call without Bach at his heels. Among his many talents, Joshua was an accomplished violinist. We accepted this as a gift, and soon he was serenading late-night outdoor dinners, such as the one in progress here.

If Joshua is expected that day, I can count on a telephone call at 4:30 A.M. "Ma'am, would it be too much trouble for you to unlock the gates? I know that key's somewhere here in my truck, but it would sure save time if I did not have to look for it."

Bach instantly falls in love with him. If Joshua goes into the office to make a telephone call, Bach is right behind him.

41

Run-in Salon

The Lambs and I are swinging along our forest path. Even in winter, a few leaves cling to the tall American beeches and oaks. Ferns peek out from heaps of crisp oak, tulip-poplar, and birch leaves. Ginastera crunches brown leaves. Saint-Saëns, Debussy, and Poulenc munch on the ferns while I sit on the poetry bench.

The treetops sway with a wavelike hum. Blue-green lichen crawls up the trunks. Today the company of these old trees and my eight beautiful lambs seeps into me with indescribable warmth. Here, amid the trees, as anyone who loves the woods knows, I feel a deep, abiding sense of belonging. I have never felt this in a city. Only here.

And just like that, the ice comes. It arrives during the night, clicking down onto the ground, collecting into a sheet as smooth as a skating pond. It was only rain at midnight, but by the time daylight unrolls across the farm, it is one solid polished mirror. The terrace is glass. On the grass, I take two steps and then slide, sitting, to the barn. I telephone Joshua. "When you pass the co-op, would you buy a big supply of straw? It looks like we ought to settle into the run-in for a time."

"You're right, ma'am, except that I don't think I'll be going today. All the roads are closed. Let's just hope the ice on the trees doesn't cut off your power. But I'll get over there as soon as I can."

The run-in is filled with clouds of fresh straw. Joshua delights in demonstrating how the old farmers at the state fair lift it with pitchforks. "The idea, see, is to let as much air as possible get in under their bodies while they lie there all day," he explains.

Mozart settles in like she's easing into a bubble bath. Bach claims a good position in the center. To Joshua's horror, I arrange bales of straw in both ends of the run-in.

"Ma'am, what are you doing? You don't plan to sit there, do you? Don't you know there are fleas in straw?"

"Oh, really, Joshua!" I make a table out of two bales. I can invite guests for tea. Saint-Saëns and Debussy lie alongside my divan. Inside the thick wall of the run-in, fortified with layers of sweaters, I spend the mornings with The Lambs, since we can't go out to walk. I know Saint-Saëns is disappointed whenever I bring along a book, and today he will have to tolerate Gustav Krist's hair-raising story of sixteen months living with nomadic Kirghiz shepherds. It would be much nicer if I would simply gaze into his eyes.

Our days begin as usual at eight o'clock with Prime Lamb and hay. Then we settle into our straw chamber. We are perfectly contented. Debussy breathes her heavy sighs. When Bach stands, long straw strands hang down around him like a hula skirt. Poulenc snuffles around for leftovers in the troughs. Mozart lies perfectly still, obviously pleased with her straw bath. Chopin stays with Charpentier.

Contained in the little shelter, we seem to blend into one another. I often wonder if they aren't somehow talking among themselves. It would not surprise me that sheep use a highly toned vocabulary of gestures such as eye signals, or even telepathy.

We humans may believe that we can't communicate with animals since we are unable to exchange spoken language with them. I know that we are capable of profound relationships with other forms of nature, but I think we have to relate to them at a level—I call it connatural—that is deeper than words. Saint-Saëns and I develop a very deep connection simply by looking into each other's faces for minutes at a time. In these uninterrupted intervals, I come to know him in a way that is completely different from knowing about him. I tend to think that the communion I develop with him is much like the knowledge I gain from centering prayer, which seems to be insight into understanding I already possess but that requires my time and attentiveness to retrieve.

My relationship with Saint-Saëns develops slowly. Day after day, he is in front of me, focusing his entire existence on mine. I look at his face. My eyes penetrate the layers of his black-and-gold eyes. Here I am in the presence of the proud lamb vitality that informs his thick, curly fleece, his voluptuous tail, and those shiny black hooves. He is Saint-Saëns all the way to the tip of his snout. There is no need for him to explain himself to me in language because his living form expresses his essential meaning more forcefully than any words could.

To truly see him, I must quiet myself; in this encounter, I am aware of my limits. I am, you could say, at my most human because I can sense how different he is from me. He reminds me of the remoteness, the mysterious grandeur of the baby lambs that first day at the breeder's farm. And yet, I feel that I am enlarged by my relation with him. Faced with this concentrated expression of his being, I respond with humility. It is a measure of the power of his lambness, of his sheepness, his eternal species inheritance. This is why The Lambs move me so deeply and inexplicably. I ask myself, In the presence of these sacred beings, is not my life judged? I think, Yes, yes.

I know that at one time I interpreted my sheep, those in the dream as well as these, who are in my care, as messengers. But the hours in the run-in have persuaded me that they are not messengers. They are the message. And it is this: Just be yourself, but be all of yourself. Live your own life as fully as you can. Look at how beautiful we are. All we do in life is be sheep.

42

Nights in the Barn

We pass through wintry February, then March. When we finally emerge from the barn, Ginastera pioneers a new trail directly to the pond. We stop at the bench. Ginastera rubs against its back until it's loose. Saint-Saëns gnaws one armrest while Bach chews the other one. Charpentier scrapes its blistered green paint with his lower teeth. I wonder why his caretaker, Chopin, tolerates this. Debussy stays beside me. She seems sluggish, as though something isn't quite right with her.

When Dr. Comyn visits, I tell him that Debussy seems out of sorts. I am supporting her while he trims her front hooves. "Is there anything wrong with her feet? She seems like she's hesitating to walk." He says to her, "Come on, little Debussy. You've got to pick up your game."

I ask, "She can't be reacting to the heat yet, can she? I don't think it's even warm."

"Not likely," he says. "We'll just have to watch her closely."

I decide to move into the barn. The loft bedroom is perfect at this time of the year. Balcony out over the pasture, cool evenings, gentle presence of The Lambs below me. But now I'm able to hear a sound that I do not like. Debussy's breathing has always been heavy, but tonight it rasps. It seems that she is struggling to inhale. How has she managed to hide this from me?

Could this be pneumonia again? Impossible. Dr. Comyn checks them at least monthly. I know her temperature is normal. I tiptoe down to where she is lying at the back of the barn. I don't think she sees me as she works to take in air. When she exhales, it sounds like a growl.

Dr. Comyn comes to examine her with the stethoscope. Nothing is blocking her lungs. She is not exhibiting any pain. He reminds me that she's seven years old. "You have got to remember that these are very old sheep for this breed," he tell me. "For any breed, as far as that goes. I think we may have a case of heat stress. Remember, she can't sweat. Sheep can eliminate internal heat only through breathing." But it isn't even warm outside.

The next day, Debussy does not leave the barn, nor does she get off the floor to eat or drink. She nibbles a gingersnap from my hand. I place a small pan of water in front of her. I sit with her all afternoon. Very occasionally, she moves. She may fold one front leg under her body and extend the other. But that's all.

Around five o'clock, Joshua sprints into the barn. "I just talked with Doc Comyn," he says. "I hear Debussy isn't well. I thought maybe I could take the other ones out for a walk."

"Oh, that's perfect," I say. "They've been in all day. I think they're getting restless."

They cluster around him and rumble out of the barn. Bach will stroll beside him, gliding along as though he's balancing a crown on his head. Ginastera will sashay in front. I can picture Mozart and Saint-Saëns on their back feet, scraping leaves off low maple branches. Fat Poulenc will scoop leaves off the ground while Charpentier lithely tiptoes beside Chopin.

Debussy doesn't even seem to notice that they're all gone. Perhaps she knows I'll stay with her. I hate to think that she doesn't care. But I am rarely alone with one of them, and, to me, this is privileged time. She drops her head onto her outstretched front leg. Long sigh. I know she hasn't eaten anything today, and she hasn't drunk anything, either. While we sit together, I talk to her. "Do you have any idea what a thrill it was to see you that first day? Do you realize you were the first lamb I ever touched? Do you remember how I would walk in and grab you and swing you onto my shoulder?"

Joshua returns with his happy troupe. They chase him to the feed closet. He sprinkles their soy-hull pellets—the protein content of their feed has been reduced for "mature" sheep—and comes over to sit beside Debussy and me. "Well, ma'am, I won't have any time to come over tomorrow because of my schedule at the dairy farm. If there's anything you want to go and do, I've got some time now and I'm happy to stay here with her."

She seems comforted by our presence. She looks up at him while I stroke her back. How grateful I am for him. He knows as well as I do that tomorrow I will be making a tough decision. After he leaves, I sit with Debussy until the sky is black. I place my face next to hers to whisper good night. She does not turn to look in my direction when I retreat to the upstairs room.

Early the next morning, my neighbor pens the other lambs into the run-in with their morning feed. All folding wooden windows are closed, central doors latched. Debussy has not shifted her position in the night. Since yesterday, she seems to have turned gray. Dr. Comyn arrives. He wastes no time. He kneels beside her to administer the injection. No one speaks. The men lift the bundle of her body, wrapped in a white wool blanket, onto the neighbor's pickup. He slowly follows Dr. Comyn up the road.

I open the run-in doors, expecting The Lambs to charge in. But they stand in a tight formation in the doorway, immobilized. Finally, Ginastera ambles over to the front of the room. He halts and stares into the corner. At the same moment, Saint-Saëns positions himself between the central pair of bifolding doors. He stands there, glaring out the glass door. Bach stations himself in the center of the room. Chopin moves over to face into the southeast corner. Rigid. Charpentier does not move from the doorway to the run-in. Poulenc and Mozart, in parallel positions a yard apart, stand in the back.

I cannot leave the barn. Whatever else I might have done to distract myself will have to wait. This is an experience I want to share with them.

At first, the barn is silent. After a while, I hear a low, steady hum. Then another voice joins at a slightly higher pitch. More voices, until there is a thick layer of sound. It is so penetrating that I hear it in my entire body.

43

In Arcadia

Nicholas Poussin forecast this day in his large canvas *The Arcadian Shepherds*, which hangs in the Louvre. Three shepherds and a shepherdess assemble around a tomb they have discovered among the trees in the legendary land where they spend their days piping tunes on their flutes. Under a sky that modulates from cloudless blue on the left to eerie dark on the right, they bend to study the inscription on the tomb, *Et in Arcadia Ego*. They gesture among themselves as they grapple with the meaning of these words.

This is their first encounter with a prefiguration of death. Poussin tells us that even in Arcadia, shepherds in the full flush of their youth must contemplate mortality. Perhaps they have assumed that the bliss of young love will last forever. Poussin insists that the ideal happiness of Arcadia can be appreciated only if a consciousness of death underlies its idyllic surroundings.

Time is flying. I have known since the beginning that the younger lambs were not likely to thrive. They were small at birth, of an unknown bloodline. First came that horrible episode with Rameau. But I had known him so little. Then tender Fauré, whose love of wooden flute music endeared him to us. But he, too, was with us for such a short time. We admired his attention to Couperin, but Ravel was always an island unto himself.

Satie was thoroughly satisfied with his one earthly friend and ignored the rest of us. Of course I miss the novelty of his fleece and regret my father's loss of his affection. We all developed a robust respect for poor Couperin. To see him strain to keep up with his flock was heartbreaking. But with these younger lambs, I never felt the bonds that have built up with the older ones.

Debussy's death strikes me with particular force. She was the foundation. My first lamb, named for my beloved composer. My daily companion, her chin resting in my left hand morning after morning. On several occasions later this year, I catch myself waiting to feel her chin slide onto my palm as we make our walks along the streambed path.

Debussy. Debussy was the first member of my flock, named for the composer who is dear to me. Even in advanced age, she had the sweetness that was part of her being when I first picked her up and carried her around the breeder's farm on my left shoulder. She was always silent and perfectly composed. She also retained the lovely apricot-tinted curls around her face that distinguished her as a very young lamb.

44

Perfect As It Is

Autumn slips into an uneventful, mild winter. Early the next year, just before the dogwoods blossom, we are happily preparing for a long visit from my father. Instead of coming almost every other month as he has in the past, he now visits about twice a year. Springtime is his favorite time to be in Virginia, and all of us—old friends from New York and Washington, and a few new local acquaintances—are looking forward to these three weeks.

He no longer makes any attempt at manual labor. I had seen enough blood running down his hands from his barbed-wire enterprise, and I am far more interested in simply being in his company than in having his help.

He sees the natural richness of the farm with true contemplative eyes. I know that the minute he picks a tiny wild violet blossom, he will observe something of the precision of its petals. Today he men-

Strolling with my father. In this picture, The Lambs and my father have walked all the way around the far end of the property and have arrived on the highest point of the ground across the road from the forest. What you do not see in this image is the level of the ground that looks down onto the scene of the front pasture. This is where the pets' cemetery lies.

tions Tennessee Williams's reference (in *Camino Real*) to the strength of the violets that grow up through the rocks.

I cannot avoid noticing that his old fingers work harder to tie his leather shoelaces. He always reaches for a walking stick when he takes The Lambs out. But every day, he greets us in his tattered old tweed coat over crisply pressed blue jeans, with a fresh white knit shirt and brilliant blue ascot. "Do it with style," he says, winking, as he pulls on his rumpled wool hat to accompany The Lambs into the field.

Later we retire to the loft bedroom to compare notes on our

Out on an investigation. Here, starting at the back of the line, you see Charpentier, Mozart, Poulenc, Ginastera, Bach, and Saint-Saëns. You will notice that in the parterre behind them there is no surrounding wire fence to challenge Charpentier. The boxwoods have been replaced with inexpensive Japanese hollies, and we have made a wire cloche to protect each plant.

studies. Since his last visit, I have acquired a first edition of Arminius Vámbéry's famous old book about the history of Bokhara. I delicately unfold the yellowed map out of it. "Here, Daddy, is the Karakul bazaar in the old town."

He studies the map for a minute. "Keep this one away from Saint-Saëns. It's a treasure." The precious lambskins were sold in a premier location near the city's principal building, the Citadel (or the Ark), the fortress of the final emirs. Directly across the street is the Mir-i-Arab Medresseh. To see its blue-tiled cupola is claimed to be an unforgettable privilege. The tall minaret of the Mir Arab was known as the "Tower of Death." From it, criminals condemned by the emirs were hurled down onto the stone pavement below.

People from all corners of the world have been attracted to Bokhara's constellation of covered bazaars. There are separate bazaars for books, gold, shoes, ironware, leather, silks, carpets, and pottery. Among them are booths where butchers, bankers, tanners, and smiths work. All together, with bakeries, restaurants, and tea shops, the marketplace occupies about a square half mile.

The great caravan city of Bokhara, the capital of the richest Central Asia khanate, is situated on an oasis and was a natural stop on the long trade routes. Although silk, with its lustrous sheen and high tensile strength, symbolized the romance of the network, the pelts of the Karakul lambs were an important component of the trading scheme.

Even when the advent of shipping forced the old camel caravan routes into gentle decline, and many of the lambskins were sent to the fur market at Nizhny Novgorod, on the east side of the Caspian Sea— or still later, when Leipzig fur specialists improved the treatment for the hides and the principal market shifted to the other side of the Caspian—the pastoralist nomads maintained their valuable flocks and continued to deliver the black lambskins to Bokhara. Despite its dilapidated state, the famous old Karakul bazaar continued to attract international fur buyers who wanted to purchase at the source.

Bokhara was not only a commercial hub. It became a renowned center of intellectual activity. Its library rivaled the "House of Wisdom" in Baghdad. Sufi mystics congregated in Bokhara, and pilgrims and scholars often followed the long-distance camel caravans. For Islam, it was considered to be a holy place; so holy, it was said, that while elsewhere on earth the daylight shone downward from the skies, from Bokhara it radiated upward to illuminate the heavens.

But the religious heritage of the area reaches much further back than the advent of Islam. Zoroastrianism, which some scholars claim was founded as long ago as 1500 B.C. in neighboring Balkh, was the first attempt to unify a religion under the worship of one supreme god. It introduced the classic conflict between good and evil in the struggles between Ahura Mazda, god of light, and Ahriman, god of darkness. Although mankind was called upon to fight for the survival of all that is light and good, Zoroastrianism provided the Fravartis as intermediary celestial beings to assist in the battle. These ancestors of our angels are the dead who choose to return to the world of the living. Each person has one of these heavenly guardians to guide him toward the realization of his higher nature.

How could we have predicted that a flock of newborn lambs would lead us into such beguiling territory? My father loves this project as much as I do. All through the day, I hear him trudging up and down the steps to the loft, whenever he is prompted to seek out another book. But I cannot help noticing that he stops to catch his breath halfway up the flight of stairs, and in the course of the next few days, we install him in his new headquarters, what we call the "Clubhouse," in the lower level. Before he returns to Montana, we organize his favorite books on shelves next to his writing table, and his farm wardrobe will be waiting for him in a closet I've painted brilliant Chinese red.

One warm summer afternoon, Joshua and I are cleaning out the hay closet in the barn. Because of the demands on his time and what I take to be a slight diffidence, we have not had much time for conversation. His attention is on his job and on each one of The Lambs. But I have listened to him roar into Le Berceau enough to be concerned about his driving speed on the lane.

"Joshua," I risk saying, "I know you have a lot of experience in the country, certainly more than I have, but do be careful driving down my lane. There's a young deer who lives along there somewhere, and I have narrowly missed her a couple times when she flew across in front of me."

He replies crisply, "Yes, ma'am," and changes the subject. He then tells me he has heard it said that there is a pattern in groups of older pets, where several often die at almost the same time. "I think we might be in a lucky streak," he says. "How long has it been since Debussy died?"

I say, "Come to think of it, it is now well over a year." I agree: There does not seem to be a single hint of a difficulty.

And then . . .

When Dr. Comyn visits later in the week, he calls me over to listen to the crunching sound coming from Chopin's rear hip joint. He says, "This is deterioration of the cartilage. It's extremely painful. We

Debussy beside the green bench at the pond. After the forest paths were established, we often made afternoon treks to the pond. It was always an experience to sit on the green bench. Typically, Ginastera rubbed his body against its back until it had to be completely replaced. Charpentier amused himself by scraping the blistered old green paint with his lower teeth. You see in this image where he has removed a patch of it, revealing an even earlier orange paint. Later on, when Charpentier began exhibiting odd behavior and blinking only one eye, Dr. Comyn had the original notion that he might be ingesting lead in his paint-scraping hobby. We performed all the tests for the presence of lead, but the paint was not the source of the difficulty.

can't let it go on." As that sad day ends, Charpentier stands forlornly at the fence, waiting for her to return.

It is impossible to attribute Charpentier's decline to this event. However, we all agree that his behavior radically changes. He becomes increasingly aloof. This is of concern in a creature who has an inbred tendency to attach to his group. Dr. Comyn begins to observe other worrying signs, such as blinking only one eye at a time, eating less and less, and visibly losing weight. Taken together, the symptoms force Dr. Comyn to conclude that there is a tumor on Charpentier's brain. "This is nothing to play with," he states quietly. My perfect white lamb.

Fall shearing, which has become an annual event, feels like a moment of reckoning. We serve sheep's cheese sandwiches cut with a lamb cookie cutter, orange juice, champagne. Joshua brings his violin. Songs float over the buzz of the electric shears. Another pair of guests perform their country clog dancing. But it is impossible to ignore that we are now shearing only five sheep.

One guest asks me, "Aren't you planning to bring in some new lambs? It would make you feel better. Your group is getting awfully small."

"No," I say. "That is not my plan. This experience is perfect as it is. I wouldn't want to try to extend it."

45

A Life of Writing

My little flock is less than half its original number, but as we have become a smaller group, we have become more tightly bonded than ever.

One afternoon, we are all out in the front pasture. While The Lambs calmly rip mouthfuls of their favorite grass, I sit on the ground to wait for them. Time passes, and I decide to simply lie on my back and look at the mist blue sky. I stretch out my arms as if I intend to embrace the scene.

I must have fallen asleep. When I open my eyes, I see a wall of woolly legs along mine. I instantly think of my delicate little fingers, there among all the sharp hooves. But The Lambs are carefully stepping around my hands, and I am enwrapped in white, beige, black, and bronze legs. They are not stationary. Bach's beige legs travel on my right side. Mozart changes place with Poulenc on my left side while Saint-Saëns and Ginastera slowly cross behind my

head. Positions continuously shift and legs rotate, but I remain surrounded.

Sheltered in my sheep, lying here with my palms wide open, I am
assailed by a thought that has been putting pressure on my mind for
the past several months, ever since I decided to make a list of ten
words that crystallize my connection to this place. Words such as
harmony and *restraint* and *délicatesse*, which honor the relationship
that has grown from walking around it for hours every day, walking
at the pace of The Lambs, learning to see with the eyes of my heart.
Later, I will have each word etched onto a chunk of stone, and three
of us, with the ever-present lambs, will lay them out as a footpath
connecting the lower pasture to the high ground where the pets'
cemetery lies. But the yearning to transpose my love of this land,
using these words—I can picture them as chapter headings in a
book—has been building up inside me.

And now, while we are all here in this remarkable configuration, I
feel that I receive a summons. I will always interpret—and remember—
this as the moment when my soul insisted that I step into the life of
writing, for which I had been in preparation all these years.

I consent to the call, absolutely. It feels as natural as the opening
of a flower.

A quick and light vibration fills my spirit. When I stand, I feel
buoyant, like a schoolgirl again. The Lambs must feel it, too. They
cavort around the pasture. From behind me, Poulenc runs between
my legs. He is too large to get through, and the next thing I know,
I am riding across the field on his back. Just before we plunge into
the forest, he puts his head down for one last gulp of orchardgrass,
and I slide back to earth.

46

Summer of Summers

October. November. Winter is gentle, and we launch into the blessings of spring with hearts of children, open to whatever happy surprises are in store.

Time stands still for the six months ahead. It is as simple as a bird's-eye view of characters in action. To seize this time from the relentless rush of days and weeks requires faith and sincerity, and I hold the fragment tenderly. I will come to look back on this summer as the pinnacle of the experience with The Lambs. A later reconstructive gaze will recognize that the fullness of this time casts a golden glow on all that follows. It is late May. It will be the summer of summers.

In two weeks, my father and his beloved personal attorney will arrive. It will be a long stay, two months for my father, two weeks for his friend. My father and I have agreed that during this time together we will look into Persian poetry. Of course I will hear a lot of the *Rubáiyát of Omar Khayyám*, which he has been reciting to me since I was a child. We promise to contribute anything else we can find.

For the first time in my life, I hear these words from him: "Have I read the what?"

"Daddy, have you ever come across the *Shahnameh*?"

"Well," he replies, "I must confess I'm not familiar with it, but if you'll give me the details, I'll buy a copy before I leave for Virginia."

I am thrilled by this opportunity. Once again we can share the farm and The Lambs. I can relax in my father's gracious presence. We will celebrate every particle of the time.

My visitors settle easily into the life of Le Berceau. The attorney takes over the loft bedroom. Daddy settles into his Clubhouse. I know it will be a wonderful sojourn when at lunch our friend does not flinch as Saint-Saëns helps himself to the strawberries on his plate. There will be no set schedules, no established plans. My father takes out his old copy of Edward Fitzgerald's translation of the *Rubáiyát of Omar Khayyám*.

Omar Khayyám is a fascinating character. In Iran, he is better known as a mathematician and astronomer. He composed tables for a calendar that are said to be more accurate than the future Gregorian. But his quatrains are quite enough for us. Why these verses became so popular in nineteenth-century England becomes a topic of daily discussion. People swooned over them; many memorized them. Were they just exotic fantasies? Did they relieve uncertainties of industrializing England?

A Persian friend tells me that when his countrymen visit graves, they usually sit and weep. But in the garden surrounding Omar

The Mule that my father loaded. Five lambs were still in great form the year my father spent most of the summer with us. It was to be the happiest time, with many festive visits from dear friends and many quiet private moments to review so many wonderful times together. It was clear that my father was moving more slowly and with some difficulty, and the dealer in the village generously loaned us this Kawasaki Mule for his use. On most mornings, the Mule was filled with books and bottles of wine and whatever else might be delightful, then edged along, completely surrounded by large sheep bodies. Sometimes, late in the day, if we were expecting guests for dinner, I would have to go out in search of this troupe, and often I would approach the most dreamy pastoral scene: my father seated in his carriage, reading some favorite poem, and The Lambs lying on the ground, completely encircling the Mule.

Khayyám's blue-domed mausoleum in Nishapur, they come with drums, violins, perhaps a little wine, and they sing, trying to imagine that the poet is there with them. The volume of *rubáiyát* becomes a permanent part of the equipment my father maintains in the back of the Mule, a country-style golf cart that the village merchant loans us. With a bottle of wine secured in the large rear compartment, he is ready for his day. After two enchanted weeks fly by, our friend returns to his law responsibilities in Montana.

The days with my dear father even out into a pastel pattern. I take The Lambs for an early-morning stroll. He rises somewhat later, to find them waiting at his door. They stay closer to the barn now that the days are becoming noticeably warmer. We select a site for our lunch together. Some days we meet at the Big Table, but we also have a favorite rock in the stream, to which we carry our lunch in a cotton knapsack. One of us almost always falls into the water. In the afternoons, he retires to his spot down by the stream to rest in the leaf shadows of the trees.

At last we venture into the *Shahnameh*. I was able to find an 1886 edition of the translation by an English father and son: the *Shahnameh*, "The Persian Book of Kings," by the great Persian poet Ferdowsi, who was born circa 940. The *Shahnameh* is said to be as important to the Persian identity as Shakespeare is to ours. The fraction of the poem in my one volume is probably no more than one-tenth of the entire work, but it is rich with reigns of Persian monarchs, affairs with women "slim as cypresses and radiant as the moon," royal courts full of music and feasting.

My father cannot put it down. Since his own copy did not arrive before he left, he is not shy about carrying mine away with him in the afternoon. The next morning, he asks me where an old book of Matthew Arnold's verse might be.

"Why do you want it, Daddy?" I ask.

He says, "I'll show you later. But you'll find it interesting."

When we meet for tea on the terrace, he reads these lines from Matthew Arnold's *Sohrab and Rustum*:

> *Through the black Tartar tents he pass'd, which stood*
> *Clustering like bee-hives on the low flat strand*
> *Of Oxus, where the summer-floods o'erflow*
> *When the sun melts the snows in high Pamere; . . .*

Then he hands me the *Shahnameh*, opened to Matthew Arnold's inspiration. Here is the heartbreaking tale of a young warrior's search for his father and his realization—too late—that he is dying from his father's attack on a battlefield beside the Oxus River. How does Matthew Arnold dress the young fighter that day? "And on his head he set his sheep-skin cap, / Black, glossy, curl'd, the fleece of Kara-kul; . . ."

The *Shahnameh* has a poignant history. Ferdowsi worked on the poem for decades, and he knew he had created a triumph. But his patron, the sultan, Mahmoud of Gazni, paid him in silver instead of the promised gold. Crushed, the poet retreated to the local bathhouse and divided it between the bath attendant and a sherbet seller. He was by then an old man. Later on, the sultan realized the greatness of the work and immediately sent the royal caravan, loaded with precious indigo, to the poet. Too late. As it entered the poet's village, it encountered Ferdowsi's funeral cortège traveling in the opposite direction.

In our very private days together, time becomes as seamlessly cyclical as my usual days with The Lambs. We are together without interruption. The freedom of these wonderfully simple days stirs in me a joy that I can much later return to, to bring back a summer of exaltation with my father and The Lambs. We have no problems to discuss, and without so much as a television at Le Berceau, we are shielded from current events.

I think we both know that this will be his last visit to Le Berceau. He is now truly frail. Watching the effort he makes to walk up a slight incline or to catch his breath, I wince at the idea of subjecting him to airport security. We never discuss this. I wonder if we are both working to shield each other—and ourselves—from the undeniable reality.

For the first time, I feel a certain tension between us. Too many things cannot be said. I resist the urge to probe into the state of his health, fearing that I might reveal too much of what I'm thinking. This makes me slightly edgy, and I find it tiring to

Lambs in the sitting room. With only five lambs, we were able to entertain them more easily inside the house. This was always hugely entertaining to our guests. The Lambs had been coming into the house since they were invited to an earlier Christmas party. They seemed to understand that special manners were appropriate, and they never caused the slightest difficulty.

keep up the pretense of being a perfect hostess when what I want to do is wrap my arms around him and make him promise never to leave.

But instead, I thank him for all the walks he took with me in the Montana woods. We would stop for a sip of water from a mountain stream. We would rarely talk. He wanted me to experience the sound of the breeze in the treetops, the squawks of the magpies, and the trills of the meadowlarks. Sharing that silence was far more memorable than conversation. But I could count on him for a few

verses of poetry. I often heard these favorite lines from Wordsworth's Immortality Ode:

> *There was a time when meadow, grove, and stream,*
> *The earth, and every common sight,*
> > *To me did seem*
> > *Apparelled in celestial light,*
> *The glory and the freshness of a dream.*
> *It is not now as it hath been of yore;—*
> > *Turn wheresoe'er I may,*
> > *By night or day,*
> *The things which I have seen I now can see no more.*

One afternoon, while we are sitting on the slope, looking out over
the pasture, he says, quietly, "Honey, there are only three things I
want you to mention in my obituary."

I've been expecting to hear something like this. "Yes, Daddy,
tell me."

"Well, I want you to mention that our family came into Virginia
in 1679 and established a plantation outside Richmond. Mention
that I am a member of the Bar of the Commonwealth of Virginia.
And also mention that Carroll College has given me the honorary
doctorate."

"Is that all?"

"Yes, I've been thinking about this for a while. I'll let you know if anything else comes to mind." He pauses. "Oh, and something else. I don't want a lot of drama. Shed a tear privately, if you must. But remember what a wonderful, wonderful life I've had with you and your mother, and think about these days here at the farm with The Lambs."

The late-July sun burns. It comes, as it usually does, with one blast of extreme heat. Dr. Comyn warns, "Miss George, this is not a good time to have an elderly person here. Sooner or later, this heat is going to catch up with him."

"Yes, I know," I say. "But I can't bear the thought of his leaving."

One morning after breakfast at the Big Table, I hear the words I dread. "You know, honey, I've been thinking. Isn't it time for me to go and let you give your full attention to The Lambs? You know they suffer in the summer. I love the heat, but this one seems like it's going to be rough, even to me." He hands me the *Shahnameh*. His own copy is waiting at home. He descends into his Clubhouse to begin preparing to leave. Our paths are about to diverge.

In front of the barn, we share a final toast with our favorite champagne. My father settles into the sedan that will carry him away. The instruction to the driver is this: "When you reach the gateposts, allow him just a glance back at us, and then speed away."

The Lambs and I follow. The driver proceeds as slowly as possible so they can nibble leaves all along the road. We arrive at the gates. My father knows that there will be no waving of arms. We stand, collected. It is time to go.

47

Ardor

Joshua installs the window fans for The Lambs. While we are in the barn together, he says he has something to tell me. "You may like to know," he says, "that I am about to make a change in my direction."

"What does that mean?"

"Well, ma'am, I don't know if you have any idea how much it costs to set up a dairy operation. I thought all along that's what I'd do. But I just can't manage the cost."

"So now what?" I ask.

"You know all about my church, I guess," he says. "We're a pretty tight community. One of the businesses that's really thriving right now is a construction company one of our elders runs. He wants me to join it."

I ask, "What do you think about this?"

"Well, ma'am, I like it. They tell me there isn't really any starting point. They're finishing up some projects right now, and it's a perfect time for me just to fit myself in with final details like putting in doorknobs and building bookcases."

"Do you know how to build a bookcase?" I ask.

"No, but I don't see why I can't learn."

～◦◦～

The late-afternoon sun on the glass doors in the barn is hotter than I can remember. I install bamboo shades. Saint-Saëns eats all the pulls. I would worry for his teeth if I didn't know how much they all like to chew olive pits. The steaming humidity is thicker than ever. Some afternoons, I cannot stay in the office. I've done everything I can for The Lambs, and I leave all the barn doors open just in case the air moves a little.

Suddenly, I hear a loud *Baa! Baa! Baa!* under my window. I look down. Saint-Saëns is pacing back and forth on the terrace below me. *Baa! Baa! Baa!* His black tongue is sticking straight out of his black mouth.

"Saint-Saëns, please go back into the barn," I plead. "I know it's hot, but at least you have the shade and the fans." He stays. I go into the kitchen for a saucepan of water, which I place on the ground in front of him. I try to lead him back to the barn. No! "Well, Saint-Saëns, do you want to sit under the oak tree? It's hot, but there's at least shade."

Now he is happy. No books, no guests. He arranges himself so close to me that I wonder how he survives the heat of his body. It may worry me that he is outside and removed from the few comforts of the barn, but he is contented. I rest my head on his back. We fall asleep.

Of course the next day, as the afternoon burns, I hear him once again—*Baa! Baa! Baa!*—under my window. Again, water in a saucepan and a nap under the old oak. And the next day. It is now 105 degrees, and he is walking up the slope into the blinding sun.

Finally, I telephone Dr. Comyn. "Dr. Comyn, every afternoon when I escape to my upstairs room, Saint-Saëns comes under my window and cries until I go down to sit with him. I hate to lock him into the barn. But do you think I ought to?"

Dr. Comyn is young but wise. His reply is, "All I can tell you is that you should never do anything to dampen ardor!"

48

Ginastera

August presses down on us. After a dawn walk with The Lambs, we settle into the barn. I work ice cubes down into their fleeces to cool their hot skin. I bathe their faces and ears with cold water. Gingersnaps offer some relief. I try to discourage Joshua from coming to sweep out the barn in this heat. But he insists. I can therefore depend on his 4:30 A.M. telephone call: "Ma'am, I don't know how this happened. I know the gate key is here somewhere in my truck."

Ginastera claims a new resting position. Why, I wonder, is he in the doorway outside the office? He has never been particularly interested in me. Moreover, he had the best place directly under the mist. But every afternoon, he lies just outside my door.

The moment I arrange my papers and books on my desk, Saint-Saëns arrives. He is the only one who eats gingersnaps in the high heat. With a mouthful of them and the assurance that I am nearby, he returns to the back corner that he and Ginastera share in winter.

"Dr. Comyn, why do you suppose Ginastera has changed places?"

"Well, that alone isn't troubling," he says. "He's probably found a little movement in the air over there."

"But," I say, "he seems reluctant to take the lead when we make our morning walk."

"Who wouldn't be in this filthy air? I've never seen anything like it. But watch him."

I'm troubled by his position outside the office door. Is he trying to tell me something? When Dr. Comyn comes later in the week, I call his attention to Ginastera.

"Just heat stress. Remember how old they all are now. He'll be fine once this weather breaks," Dr. Comyn explains. "Some of them do better with the heat than others." But Ginastera is our engine.

It is unavoidable: Ginastera hesitates before plowing up the slopes. More alarming is that he is the last to leave the barn in the mornings. Somehow, by the time we arrive at the entrance to the forest, he steps into his place to lead. But he is making an effort, and his natural Latin rhythm is drained out of him. I have always loved his vitality. Now I admire him for his determination. I ask Dr. Comyn once again if there isn't something we can do for him. "I'm sure it's just the heat," he says. "What can we expect? It's been one hundred degrees for ten days now."

But I'm not convinced. "Dr. Comyn, I think we really ought to look into this," I insist. We perform the usual preliminaries. We watch him walk across the floor of the barn. We make him trudge up the slope toward the house. We draw blood samples. Then Dr. Comyn has a fresh idea. "Why don't we see whether he responds to acupuncture? I know several vets who are getting some impressive results with large animals."

The acupuncturist arrives with a bag full of large needles with red yarn in their eyes. We maneuver Ginastera into the office and close the door. I hear Saint-Saëns's hooves on the floor as he paces outside. Ginastera never winces when the needles are threaded through the long wool on his back. He is the perfect patient. Needles removed, we schedule the next treatment.

The next day, he moves with greater ease. Sadly, on the second day, the benefit has worn off. We proceed with the next treatment. Again, there is visible improvement for one day. One day? I notice that he doesn't want to walk up the incline to the house. When the others go up there to nibble grass, he waits by the water. Joshua stands with him and scratches his back. We shake our heads. How can this be? This is our leader.

Acupuncture treatments that provide relief for one day are not practical. The blood profile reveals nothing. Dr. Comyn explains that one of several conditions might be the cause of Ginastera's difficulty. There is always the possibility of a tumor. Perhaps it is discospondylosis, a condition that develops when two lumbar vertebrae grow together and swelling puts pressure on nerves coming off the spinal column. Or Ginastera might have a slipped disk. But considering his age, any of these conditions would not be likely to improve. Yet Ginastera is not grinding his teeth. And he is eating.

Ginastera. Ginastera always kept a watchful eye on his twin brother, Saint-Saëns, but he never formed a close bond with any of the people who were regularly around him. He was not shy; he was always in the center of any activity but did not attach himself to any other person. His character was so strong that he was able to maintain his position as the leader of his flock with very little effort, and apparently his personality did not require any further expression.

It is early October now. Today, Ginastera will not leave the barn. He does not walk to the feed trough. He does not get off the floor. It is still often warm, but many days are noticeably cooler. If only we can hurry into the crisp days of autumn, perhaps he will once again be jumping in the air for the sheer joy of being alive.

It is not to be. Saint-Saëns hovers over Ginastera. "Dr. Comyn," I say, "I am worried about Saint-Saëns. If we decide we have to euthanize Ginastera, do you think we will also lose Saint-Saëns?"

"Well," he says, "I can't promise you anything. They do die of grief. I've seen it in the beef cows. They get really despondent if, say, one loses a calf, or a friend. These guys have close pals within the herds, you know. They may get over it, but I can promise you, they feel it. But remember, he has you. And he may be more independent than you think. I just don't know if we have any alternative. The condition is likely to get worse, and we have cold weather up ahead."

I struggle with these words. "Isn't there anything we can do for him?" I ask.

"Well, I suppose we can keep him on some kind of medication. But the effects of that will wear off in a while, and we are back to where we are. It's a shame to keep them all caged in the barn because he won't go out. I guess if he completely stops eating, we'll have to deal with it. We don't have to do anything yet."

Waiting, and uncertainty. After a week of staying in the barn with Ginastera, a certain pall spreads over the entire group. Weary from the heat and humidity of the summer, The Lambs mill around aimlessly.

Ginastera may nibble grass during the night, but I observe no eating during the day. I know it cannot go on. My fear is for Saint-Saëns.

On the selected day, we simply close the bifolding doors behind Ginastera's station outside the office. He makes no effort to move. I stay on the other side of the doors with Saint-Saëns. He knows exactly what is happening. He attends to every muffled sound. Dr. Comyn and Joshua slowly carry Ginastera's body through the glass doors and around to the front to lay him in the bed of the pickup.

I know very well that farms are places where birth and death are everyday events and that no guilt attaches to killing. But I feel a sense of outrage this time.

49

Saint-Saëns

There is no time to indulge in these thoughts about Ginastera's death. Saint-Saëns stands beside me, broken. He hears the trucks slowly grind up the gravel road. He understands the meaning of this departure. He refuses a palliative gingersnap. He slumps down against the wall outside the barn office. He pulls his legs under him. He is stone.

I sit down on the floor beside him. The Persian history of the Karakul sheep telescopes into the woolly lump huddled into the floor to seek sanctuary from a cruel, unrecognizable world. Is it better to let Saint-Saëns follow Ginastera to a better place? Ought I stay beside him while he tries to reconfigure life without his twin brother? Does he need privacy? How do I defend my belief that he will eventually accept his loss?

I am unable to bear the thought of losing Saint-Saëns. "Dr. Comyn, what do you honestly think about Saint-Saëns?"

"Well, this is a major blow to him. He will decide what he wants to do, and he'll let us know. It's possible he'll pull himself through. Remember, he has you. And there are other sheep. He may decide that he wants to survive, even after something like this. We ought to give him some time."

Books stay closed, and I sit on the floor beside Saint-Saëns. I'm not with him without a break day after day. But I am beside him for long periods of time. He no longer gazes into my face. He doesn't focus his eyes on anything. Much of the time, he keeps his eyes closed, even if his head is upright.

I place both my palms onto his back as lightly as possible. I want him to feel my presence. I run my fingers down his left ear. I love the shining black curls that have the luster of a year-old lamb's. I inhale his caramel scent. You might think that with all the other barn smells—the pine sawdust and the fresh hay bales and the other sheep—it would be impossible to distinguish his scent. But it is permanently pressed into my memory during these hours when I sit and caress his head and skim my hands down his back and simply breathe him in.

I never telephone Dr. Comyn from the barn office. Saint-Saëns must not overhear our conversations. Today I ask, "How long do you think we ought to let Saint-Saëns suffer like this?"

"Let's give it two weeks" is his advice.

I mark off the days on the office calendar. Eight. Nine. Ten. Eleven days. Saint-Saëns makes not the slightest effort to move from his sepulchre against the wall. He seems unaware of my presence. He is encrusted in darkness. Alone. I sit with him and wonder if I'll ever have him back again, or if I've lost him to the annihilating shadow in which he is engulfed.

What is going on in his mind? Has it shut down in order to survive? To me, this is precious time. Here on the barn floor, we are on common ground. While he rearranges his entire world around the loss of Ginastera, I want to believe that a fresh link, invisible yet tenacious, is binding me to him. Today, once again, we sit inside his impenetrable sadness.

And yet, of all the times I have shared with Saint-Saëns, this is the most vital. Here on the floor, we occupy an unforgettable time and place. Those who have loved someone like this will understand. There is a heightened sense of clarity, of being real and perceiving the real. The red ocher wall, the glossy black floor molding, the pine shavings, the spiderweb in a crack—it is all indelible.

I force myself to admit that I may be surrendering my best friend to an infinite gloom. No fortune, no success, nothing can be exchanged for his faithful companionship. Forever watching me, mindful of my every movement, always happy to see me, making me laugh. If he is reduced to nothing without Ginastera, how poor would I be without him? Today we sit.

⌒

Twelve days. Not that we will take any action on precisely the fourteenth day.

But, then, thirteen. Saint-Saëns must be going out into the paddock at night to nip a little grass. He can drink at the run-in waterer. Dr. Comyn agrees that he can't possibly survive with neither food nor water. I leave a small bowl of grain in front of him. I like to think that a little is missing by the afternoon. Very occasionally, Bach walks over to touch his nose to Saint-Saëns's head. He could be helping himself to a few bites. There is always Poulenc, who might dip into this extra supply. But Poulenc and Mozart stay well away from Saint-Saëns.

⌒

It is the fourteenth day. I wake very early, about three o'clock. Do we really have to deal with Saint-Saëns's destiny today? I must be with him this morning, with all of The Lambs. I enter the barn. I'm weary.

Saint-Saëns greets me at the door with the lightest little head butt on my knees. He is subdued, but he is here. Am I dreaming? I follow him over to the feed closet, where the others wait. I get a scoopful of soy-hull pellets in a new orange plastic scoop that Joshua brought in to cheer us. Saint-Saëns plunges his snout into it. Bach nudges him out of the way and takes a gulp. Poulenc waddles over for his turn, and Mozart presents her lovely self. Just before seven o'clock, I telephone Dr. Comyn. Then I telephone Joshua. "On your way to work, could you swing past the village florist for us? Go to the back door. She'll be in there. This is important. Bring me fourteen of the most beautiful roses. For Saint-Saëns."

I offer the velvety blooms to Saint-Saëns. He devours them, leaving a couple of petals stuck in one corner of his mouth. Bach, Mozart, and Poulenc nip a few of the dark, shiny leaves. Then Joshua flings open the heavy front doors for the first time in weeks. We turn to each other with triumphant smiles.

In one cluster, we proceed slowly up the road to the forest. No one leads. No one knows what to do. The Lambs spread out into a sort of wing pattern. Saint-Saëns and then Poulenc are on my right. Bach clings to Joshua, with Mozart beyond him. Soon we'll see who leads us through the wood.

Part Three

COMMENDATION

Completing the Call

50

Life Without Ginastera

Four sheep and two people enter the forest on the first day without Ginastera's leadership. The Lambs spread out to nip the lower branches of the dogwood trees. Bach tugs at a hickory sapling while Poulenc and Mozart browse among the grasses, waiting, I suppose, for Ginastera to shake his red head in the direction of the path and begin their trek. Joshua and I stand back to see who will lead. As Bach calmly walks to the front, Joshua grins at me like a proud father. Indifferently, Saint-Saëns, then Mozart, and finally fat Poulenc follow.

We walk past Christmas ferns and pine seedlings. There are enough dried oak leaves already on the ground to amuse Saint-Saëns and Poulenc. Our progress is predictably slow. At the poetry bench, the path flattens out to cross the lower section of the wood. We are about to make the turn into the pasture toward the Big Table, when Bach abruptly halts. They all stop, almost piling up on one another.

"So, Joshua, what's the problem?" I ask.

"I don't know, ma'am. But you'd better go up there and lead for a while."

With that, I walk around to the front. I get all the way to the opening onto the field. They do not budge. "Come on, Bach. Bring them over here to me. We have to finish our walk," I plead. I wait. "Well, I guess we don't have to finish our walk today," I conclude. I return to my place behind Poulenc.

The Lambs reshuffle. Bach again leads. Now they don't run, but they head straight for the barn. Joshua says, "Well, you have to realize they're adjusting to a major change. I can hardly imagine how it feels without Ginastera. I guess we ought to be grateful Saint-Saëns has himself together."

The next morning, I say to The Lambs, "Well, let's try it again." I open the heavy front doors and, just like yesterday, we proceed up the road in our new formation. We enter the wood, they scout around for leaves, and then Bach lifts his head as though he is straightening a jacket on his shoulders and leads his little group down onto the path. Once again, The Lambs nibble ferns and dried leaves, and we slowly worm along.

At the poetry bench, I stand back to watch. This is what they do. They all follow Bach until he reaches the place where they halted yesterday. They stop, reverse, and then trot to the barn. Perhaps without Ginastera and with so few of them, they feel insecure, even on their old path. We can resume our walks in the spring.

The Lambs and I now revise our morning schedules. Instead of spending all morning strolling through the pastures with them, I dedicate several hours to writing. They seem perfectly content to hover around the glass doors while I sit at my table. Mozart, Poulenc, and Bach settle down against the doors. They look out across the fields at whatever Canada geese or crows might be passing through. Saint-Saëns stands faithfully at the door to observe my every move. I can feel his eyes as I walk over to my stacks of books on the piano, and when I take a break and go out to greet them, he turns around in happy circles, so delighted by my presence.

The hours of writing each morning have filled me with a satisfaction that is entirely new. Perhaps this is the felicity that Plotinus says belongs to any life that is attaining its proper term of fulfillment. Not only do I accept this time as a privilege; I consider writing to be the greatest gift I have ever received. It is mine to foster and protect by removing obstacles and noise.

During these years, I know that I have joyfully absorbed the sweetness of all the earthly things around me—the fields, the stream, the trees, of course, The Lambs. But I also recognize how much the years have changed me, what I want to do, what I value. The presence of The Lambs has wholly supplanted any desires for long trips to foreign cities, even my favorites, Paris and London. The almost liturgical ritual of my days glistens with a jewel-like radiance that makes the thought of an airport simply offensive. Now I am not only the guardian of all that is here; I feel I am also the instrument. What can be a greater source of rejuvenation than to share my life of tranquillity with readers who are trying to survive in this modern world that is longing for unity, beauty, and peace?

Walks with The Lambs are over. We stay together for hours every day, reclining on the hillside beside the house. With the accumulation of all these quiet hours with The Lambs, I realize how deeply I understand them. In the *Timaeus*, Plato suggests that it is my contemplative life that allows me to resonate to The Lambs at this profound level. He says that when the human spirit is in harmony with itself, it is, at the same time, in harmony with the intelligence of nature.

51

Fanita

Joshua, would you like a little extra project?" I ask one morning.

"Sure. What've you got in mind?"

"I'm wondering if you could arrange a couple extra hours one day. You know that slope across from the forest—it always looks so messy—you know the one I mean? On the right side of the road, as you're going down the hill. Could you just rake the leaves out of there?"

The next week, I'm away one entire day. When I return, there's a puzzling telephone message from Joshua. He is apologizing for ruining the big drop cloth and a couple of my heavy rakes. This makes no sense. There could not possibly have been enough leaves on that little hillside to cause all this damage.

"Well, ma'am," he explains when I return his call, "I had to go get two other boys to help me. There was no way I could do all that by myself." He had completely misunderstood the instruction. My back aches when I realize that he and his two friends have raked all the leaves from one entire side of the forest!

"Joshua, I think we need to talk," I say. "Let's not go into it right now, but I would never have asked anyone to rake the interior of the forest. What were you thinking?"

I'm thinking about the best way to be fair and to preserve a valuable relationship, when Joshua announces that there is nothing to discuss. He says to me, "Ma'am, you will not be paying me anything for this. I completely didn't listen to you. It's on me." We work out a compromise. But gone is the scrawny "kid" who came to sweep out the barn. Standing in front of me is a man of substance, looking me straight in the eye, claiming responsibility for an error.

I am not surprised to receive another telephone call from Joshua later that month. He says, "Ma'am, can I come over to see you Saturday afternoon?"

"Yes, of course, Joshua, that would be lovely."

He then says, "There's someone I'd like to introduce to you."

"And what is her name?" I ask.

On Saturday, I meet Fanita, who has brown eyes into which I could look forever and who possesses the self-confidence that can come only from supreme self-discipline. If the skinny kid is long gone, so, too, is the boy with whom any attempt at conversation ended in either "Yes, ma'am" or "No, ma'am."

Today he cannot stop talking. He describes the house he is going to design and build for them, and then he starts telling me about her cooking. I think this might go on all afternoon, but Fanita interrupts to remind him that if he wants the apple cake she has promised for dinner, it is time to leave.

52

Talk of the Past Then, Tenderly

In the early evening, I decide to retrace our old route through the wood. I may as well learn how it feels to walk on it by myself. I pass the open doors of the barn. No one follows.

As I enter the forest, I see not a single cloud above the tops of the trees. It brings to mind the glorious November afternoon just three years ago when we laid out these paths, The Lambs leading as I followed along behind with enough blue plastic flags to mark the trail they found between stops to eat leaves. Then my father arrived. How would I ever forget the sheen of joy on his face—which ought to have been weary from twelve hours of travel—when I proposed creating a monument to poetry.

I proceed to the poetry bench. This is where I talk with him. I can see in my mind's eye his old green hat above the woolly mass of The Lambs crowding around him. What do they want now? The feather in his hatband? His hat? Of course, the gingersnaps in his lunch sack. And here he is, with his old stiff fingers trying to disentangle the damp pages of his favorite poems, which are glued together by moisture and rust.

Somewhere high above me, in the top of an old tulip-poplar, an invisible yellow-billed cuckoo is singing his desolate song. It is the perfect background music for Petrarch's Sonnet 307. I lift the lid of the candy tin and peel apart the fragile page of that verse. I can hear so clearly my father's voice reading the poet's invitation to a "lovely little bird" to come and sit with him to share their sadness: ". . . let us talk of the past then, tenderly."

I am drawn to this place, but I must go feed The Lambs. I must go down to the basement to make sure all the lights are off. I must. I must.

I must sit here a little while longer and feel the surface of this bench where I sat with my father while he read to me. I must stay in this place and remember the sight of him leading eight sheep across the pasture, in those days when he walked with only the support of a walking stick, when there were sheep willing to venture out.

Is today, I ask myself, is today the day that I must face the reality that time here is drawing to a point, that the time with The Lambs is tapering, that the time with my dear father is funneling down?

Oh, but not today. Perhaps I will be granted a little while. My father will return for another visit in the spring. The Lambs will resume their morning walks. And everything will be as it has been, everyone carrying on as though there is no such thing as age or time or death, as though there is no weary succession of nights and days and no obstinate demands of the months and the years.

No, I must believe that all is as it ought to be, from sunset to sunrise, all in perfect order, even though now I can sense a rotation of the scene that began with the ceremonious departure of my dear father and the conclusion of the life of our leader, Ginastera.

Saint-Saëns. This is the face of my dear Saint-Saëns, who greeted me with a friendly head butt against my knees when I entered the barn and who vigilantly watched my every move when I was within his sight. His ears are long, a characteristic of the Karakul breed. In this image, you can see that there is a diamond of white hair on his snout and a little more white under his chin. This bothered all of us, because Saint-Saëns, more than any of the others, retained such a youthful spirit, and it seemed incomprehensible that he would ever show any hint of age.

53

The Prettiest Feet

My gentle afternoons in the barn office reading Persian poetry and fending off Saint-Saëns are over. Since those Thursdays when he waited during Ginastera's acupuncture treatments, Saint-Saëns has not stepped across the threshold. How he must have suffered out there. If I reach forward from where I sit, he will snatch a gingersnap from my hand. But no amount of coaxing draws him in.

This is not to suggest that Saint-Saëns shuns me. He is attached to me as if he were an appendage. Wherever I am, he is. The moment I sit somewhere for a cup of tea, he is there. This enables him to demonstrate his new skill: He positions himself directly in front of me and then presents one of his front feet for me to shake. Just like a dog.

"Yes, Saint-Saëns, you have the prettiest feet," I say as he lifts his perfect black hoof for me to hold or to admire as it rests on my knee.

When Dr. Comyn sees this performance, he can't help saying,

"You realize, no 'normal' sheep owner would believe this! Sheep just don't do stuff like that."

Saint-Saëns lovingly lays his front hoof in my lap and gazes into my eyes.

I cannot help noticing the white hair that covers his snout. Joshua had laughed about a few white hairs on his nose during the summer, but now there is a solid white beard under his chin, clumps of white on either side of his mouth, and a diamond of bright white on his nose. None of this was there when we sat together on the floor of the barn. If this is a sign of how he feels without Ginastera, I wonder how he is able to absorb his loss.

As though he is reading my thoughts, Dr. Comyn says, "You know, I hate to say this to you, but this place just isn't right without Ginastera."

"It makes me wonder how Saint-Saëns is managing," I say. "Dr. Comyn, have you noticed that the hair on his face has turned white?"

"It bothers me so much," he says, "that I haven't been able to say anything about it."

54

Never Fewer Than Four

Now the breeder's words echo in my head. *You cannot have fewer than four. They are flocking creatures. Never fewer than four. Preferably from their bloodline. At least from their breed.* If four is the absolute minimum, what do I think I'm doing? I now have four elderly sheep in my care. What should I be doing about their futures? There is no time to waste.

I begin by visiting several local farms that have Karakul sheep from my breeder. There is financial strain at the first farm, and the boarding fee they propose is so astronomical that I politely flee. There is another farm across the river. But here the young owner, who began his flock with about as many sheep as I had originally, has developed a major business, supplying meat to restaurants all over the Mid-Atlantic region. "I've always loved your sheep, but I just can't handle any more," he says. Thank goodness. I can't imagine my precious four sheep in that mob.

But I am constantly thinking, What is best for The Lambs? Should they be with other animals? Or, on the other hand, would any move be too traumatic for them at this point in their lives? And what if something happened to me? At least I need an emergency plan.

My father's Montana attorney friend agrees to be the legal guardian of "his lamb nephews." This is the first major step.

Then I ask Dr. Comyn what he would suggest as an emergency home for them. His response is, "Hell, I'll just take them over to my place."

The attorney and I establish the "Lamb Account" at my village bank. It is, not surprisingly, the first lamb trust fund, and there's a lot of giggling at the bank while I fill out the forms. To fund the account, I search through my closet for Chanel suits. These sleek black pieces, part armor and part fashion during my working days, were an excellent investment. They resell handsomely at a consignment store in New York, and the lamb fund is flush.

Emergency plans in place, I revisit the more pressing concern of a home for The Lambs. A friend suggests an organization in upstate New York that rescues farm animals. I immediately telephone the Farm Sanctuary, but I know there is no way I would truck them all the way north. Moreover, how can I presume to place four pet sheep in a shelter that is more than overcrowded due to the unfathomable barbarity of man to beast?

"Donate to Help The Lambs!" reads their most recent newsletter. "Found motherless, cold and starving in central New York, the suckling babies were the only survivors out of a group of 20 helpless animals who were purchased and left to fend for themselves in a frightening, lonely world. . . ."

Waiting for their afternoon walk. Four lambs are waiting for me to take them on a brief walk that does not go too far from the house or the barn. For some reason, Mozart is not visible in this picture. She was the one who had figured out how to manipulate the lever door handles, which were the same on the exterior as you see here. She must have watched how I opened the doors, because she developed this skill rather early. That day, I was in the music room, on the other side of the house, practicing the piano. At a stopping point, I was aware of an unusual sound in the small sitting room that you see in this image. I was a bit surprised to see Mozart standing in the center of the room, as though she had been patiently waiting for me to take a break from practicing.

There are, however, satellite sanctuaries around the country. There are a few near here, and my neighbor offers to help me explore them. But every rescue farm is beyond its capacity. One owner says she *might* be able to adopt *one* of mine.

"Dr. Comyn, I know you agreed to take in The Lambs in an extreme emergency. What if they moved over there now so they would have your dogs and horses to play with? People keep telling me I ought to get them with other animals, even if they're not sheep."

"Wow. Interesting. Let me give it some thought."

The concept must have merit, because on his next visit he says that he has located an ideal place for a little sheep shelter. It has a water hydrant and an electric hookup. "Have you given any thought to a floor plan?" I ask. "My contractor is busy, and we ought to get moving."

"Here's my thinking so far," he says. "The main concern is protecting them from the heat. That's more important in Virginia than worrying about the cold. The trick will be to figure how to ventilate it." Now every time Dr. Comyn visits, he comes with a new proposal for the layout. He designs an interior that gives each sheep far more space than he says is recommended. Then he lays out a clever placement of walls that allows easy traffic flow as well as protection from the wind. And he delights me with a sample of heavy canvas, which he proposes to roll at the ceiling and lower to protect from sun and rain.

One morning, my neighbor and I are sitting in the barn. "So what do you think about Dr. Comyn's plan?" I ask.

"Oh, it's all very interesting, but you know as well as I do that The Lambs aren't going anywhere," he replies. "If Saint-Saëns went out of here, you'd be right behind to bring him back. Just hunker down right here. This is home."

"Yes," I say, "but what about their refusing to walk in the mornings? We all agree they're insecure because their group is so small. If they go over to the Comyns' farm, they'll have other animals. And don't forget there are two vets in the household."

"I don't care what you say." He chuckles and adds, "It'll never happen."

55

The Fence

Out of the blue, the woman who made the hat from Rameau's wool telephones to ask if she can come to see me. "Of course," I reply, "but I don't have any more wool." She says, "No, but I'm going to be down your way. There's something I ought to tell you. I know how careful you are with your little group."

She begins, "We know some people who have a few sheep. They always go away to ski in the winter, but they've always left them in the care of a next-door neighbor. Apparently, there was a new family down the road. They knew they had a German shepherd, but the people thought they could trust their chain-link fences." I don't like this story.

"Well, anyway, the German shepherd found a Labrador somewhere, and they worked a hole into the fence. One of the sheep got out. Two sheep were just mauled. Really gross. One somehow survived until the neighbors heard all the barking and got hold of the dogs."

What is there to say? Isn't this exactly what all sheep owners fear the most?

I locate a bottle of sherry and two little glasses and try to end the conversation by thanking her for coming with this news. I take it to heart.

I immediately telephone Dr. Comyn. "Is the ground too frozen to dig fence postholes?"

"I wouldn't think so," he says. "It never freezes more than three inches down, and any drill can get through that." He comes to consult. "You can't be too careful," he agrees. He recommends a small high-security enclosure attached to the run-in. "Make it at least seven feet high. Put in five-inch-round poles—no more than seven feet apart—and use a narrow gauge of wire, like two inches by four inches. Then run your electric wire about every ten inches. Have the bottom strand three inches above the ground. And I'd run a string of wire on the inside, three inches off the ground."

The local fencing contractor is happy with a midwinter job, and the fence is completed within weeks. I sprinkle bits of bread on the tops of the posts, and already birds are chirping on the top wire. I know that we have reinforced our security, but in truth I think we've created a prison yard.

My sentiment is shared. Saint-Saëns, Bach, Poulenc, and Mozart stand side by side in the run-in door, glaring at the fence. No one steps into the paddock. I pace around the inside. Alone.

"Yes," agrees Dr. Comyn when he comes to admire the impene-

Saint-Saëns. The Lambs hated the tall fence around the security paddock so much that they never ventured into the area. We tried to think of ways to entice them out of the run-in, but with no success. Finally, I suggested a bench swing that could be suspended from the huge beam of the run-in roof. The first sound of the clanking of the chain sent Poulenc off in a fright. Not even a handful of gingersnaps would entice them near the swing, which I happened to love. Occasionally, my faithful Saint-Saëns would deign to join me near it. I appreciated the sacrifice this entailed, because I knew well that they all found the swing an appalling intrusion into their territory. The dreaded tall fence, and then this thing.

trable fence, "I can see it has definitely interfered with their view of the universe."

"Dr. Comyn, if I make a project of spending more time out here, do you think they'll accept it?"

"Oh, it might help. But you stay away from it. It's meant to keep out a mountain lion."

56

Home

Restlessness in the barn is the first sign of spring. Birdsong breaks out in a frenzy, there is a fever of rebuilding nests, and swallows are skimming everywhere. At the pond, turtles dive underwater at a stranger's approach. A heron arrives to stand vigilantly on one leg, like a stork.

One afternoon, I receive a telephone call from a new acquaintance in Vermont who also has a small flock of sheep. Hers are Merinos, her own supply of knitting yarn. She has had sheep for quite a long time, maintaining her number by frequent lambing.

Today she tells me that she's about to be in my situation. She's decided to move across the country to be near her son and will be letting her flock die out. She has talked with a number of farmers who've faced this juncture and hasn't yet heard of any really good solution.

"But one thing is for sure," she says. "Everyone I talk with says you absolutely cannot have one sheep. You aren't thinking about doing that, are you? I know how close you are to yours, but believe me, I've heard of some real tragedies."

"No," I tell her. "I can't picture it. My four seem really insecure. They don't even want to go out to walk around much beyond the barn area."

And then I tell her about Rameau's anguished call—the only sound I ever heard him make—when he was too sick to stand and the others were moving out of his sight for a little exercise.

After we promise to stay in close touch, I remember the breeder's admonition, *You cannot have fewer than four*, which plays in my mind like a recording. Now it has been replaced by *You cannot have one sheep.*

I comprehend the reasons for sparing one of my old sheep the agony of being the lone survivor of his flock. And yet I have my conscience—and my heart—to answer. One of them would die what could be characterized as an unnecessary death. Am I, I ask myself, about to perform some version of ritual sacrifice?

When Dr. Comyn comes the next time, I ask, "Have you given any more thought to moving The Lambs over to your farm?"

"Say, you know, I'm sorry," he says. "I keep meaning to talk with you about it. I've gone over it a lot, and you know how much I'd like to have these guys over there. But I still have one major concern."

"What is it?" I ask. "I've been wondering why we aren't getting anywhere."

"The more I think about it, the more I worry about putting them in with my young heifers."

"Why would they be a concern?" I ask.

"Well," he says, "my girls would almost certainly chase them. They'd think they were playing, but they could really upset—or, more likely, injure—these sheep. You ought to see them. It wouldn't be anything personal. They're certainly not malicious. But think about eight-hundred-pound animals that want to play with you."

I'm speechless. "Eight hundred pounds?"

"Easily. And they play pretty rough."

"Well, I thought your little building sounded so interesting. But we aren't going to take that sort of risk. And, Dr. Comyn," I assure him, "to tell you the truth, I know there are plenty of reasons against keeping them here, but that's really what I want to do. I know what's ahead. What if Saint-Saëns were the final unlucky one? But I know you'll stand by me and that we'll do all the right things at the right times. And I truly believe that everybody ought to stay right here."

Is it just plain selfish to keep them here? Am I condemning them to miserable old age by clinging to them? Or would a move destroy all the stability of their lives? This is their home, after all, as much as it is mine. And where would they go?

Dr. Mary Midgley insists that to acknowledge an animal's species is absolutely essential to his well-being, that beyond different basic needs regarding temperature, water supply, bedding, and space, each has its unique vision and experience of the world. These differences are real and need to be respected. I can't ignore the breeder's command that sheep need to be with other sheep. Or at least with other animals. Dr. Midgley concurs. She writes that if a grazing animal is left alone in a field, he grows uneasy and depressed.

Mozart. Mozart is simply lovely, as she knows perfectly well. From her first day on this earth, she was thoroughly convinced of her distinct grace, and she never wavered in that belief. She did, however, sleep with her chin on Bach's back, and at times it seemed that she had accepted Poulenc into her very private existence. As for the rest of us, she tolerated us, to a certain degree.

57

The Month of May

It is warm enough for me to sleep in the loft. Along the ledge at the head of the bed are framed photographs of The Lambs. Vibrant-colored yearling bodies around the red metal hayrack at the old white shed. Eleven sheep posed on the grass for our Christmas card that year, "Peace on Earth." My favorite hazy golden scene of The Lambs and my father on the first day we took them out to the front pasture. Another shows a wedge of six sheep, Ginastera in front, Bach and Saint-Saëns behind him on one side, Charpentier and Poulenc on the other, with Mozart floating in the distance.

I tiptoe down the stairs to observe my four sheep, settled in for the night. Bach softly snores. Mozart's chin rests on his back. Saint-Saëns, forever on the alert, notices me but, fortunately, does not jump up. Poulenc lugubriously looks in my direction but does not attempt to lift his majestic body. The sight of the four is jolting. Not so long ago the run-in was alive with woolly activity. Even during the winter, with all the straw furniture, it was lively. To-night four sheep are limned against the starry country sky. Lonesome, tired, old.

And then our little world shrinks.

Mozart falls during a scuffle at the feed trough. She gnashes her teeth in unbearable agony until Dr. Comyn arrives.

Not two weeks later, before we've even retrieved Mozart's ashes from the funeral home, Dr. Comyn and I are standing in the barn, watching Bach, Saint-Saëns, and Poulenc crowded together at a feed trough.

With no warning, both of Poulenc's rear legs give out at the same time, and he tumbles onto the floor.

Without hesitation, Dr. Comyn declares: "Okay. Central nervous system. Could be a tumor. Maybe a blood clot. Doesn't matter. Bad news."

Dr. Comyn euthanizes Poulenc where he lies on the floor. There is something irreverent in all this. What is happening? It's all too fast. Too much to take in. Two sheep is not a flock.

As soon as three men load Poulenc's body into the back of my neighbor's truck, Dr. Comyn comes over to where I am standing with Saint-Saëns and Bach.

"Look," he says. "You can't have remorse over this. You can regret it all you want, but that isn't going to change anything. You really have to face where we are. And that reminds me, since our last conversation, I read of an experiment I need to tell you about. They put individual sheep in separate pens, where they couldn't see each other. Apparently, they got very agitated and weird."

"What do you mean 'weird'?"

"You know, it's just that it isn't right to keep one by himself. Remember, sheep are prey animals. They rely on one another to be on the lookout. If there aren't others around them, the level of discomfort can be high. That group is their security."

I thank him for that and assure him I will not take that risk. There will be only one more occasion such as this morning.

Then he says, "I know how you feel. But, look, they've had a pretty good life over here, and they've far exceeded their life expectancy. This is an inevitable part of having pets."

The four of us slowly walk over to the door. Saint-Saëns is tightly wedged between us. Bach, straight and noble, is on his other side. Dr. Comyn places one hand on Bach's head and one on Saint-Saëns's. Looking out toward the trees at the edge of the stream, he makes a final statement. His words will resonate for years: "Any relationship is about knowing that at the end there's a separation. For all the pleasure, you always know that there will be pain at the end. That is where the beauty of it comes from."

58

Noon Peace

Bach and Saint-Saëns and I resume our sheer joy of living. We may have glimpsed the divine threshold, but oh, the hours and the days—and, as it will turn out, the ten months we will have together. June rolls out its long, lush green carpet in front of us. There will be no long absences or extended visits. Just uninterrupted hours in the beauty of Le Berceau.

Ahead of us is a moderate summer but for one inexcusably hot August week, a mild winter, for which no one so much as dons a heavy coat. The stream continues to meander around Le Berceau until it leaves to meet the Chesapeake Bay. The Lambs will one day ascend to the pets' cemetery to rejoin their flock. I have these tender months in which to quietly cast off my role as shepherdess and prepare to reclaim my place in the wider world. I now follow my precious creatures, once objectified in the cults of the old religions, back toward their upward spiral of dazzling white light.

There are days when I am tempted to feel sad because our world here has so drastically shrunk. But I don't achieve it. As soon as I go down to the barn to feed Bach and Saint-Saëns, all sense of anxiety or loss flees. How can I feel anything but gratitude for all that this place and these lambs have given to me? There is perhaps a temptation to declare that the country is no longer country, all cleaned and clarified. That the sheep are no longer sheep, having been reduced to pets who politely join tea parties on a countryside lawn. But not so fast!

The Lambs are sniffing the fresh morning air that billows through the barn as I walk down to decorate the gateposts with wildflower bouquets to greet afternoon guests. Persuaded that Bach and Saint-Saëns will never again go beyond the barn, I do not so much as tie ribbons around the flowers in advance.

As soon as I reach the flat lower stretch of road, I hear the sound of gravel pouring onto a surface. At the crest of the slope, Bach's hooves are four inches deep in the new top dressing of pinkish beige gravel. Saint-Saëns's black ears flap at his back. What happened to the sheep who wouldn't set foot outside the paddock? I charge up to them and slow my pace so they can nip ferns all along the road.

At the gateposts, I quickly tie my bows. Luckily, I'm skilled at dodging Saint-Saëns. And from now on, Bach and Saint-Saëns join every recitation of poetry, every piano recital, every tea party, and every other transparent, sensuous, and melodious particle of life at Le Berceau.

If the days lack the old intensity of Ginastera's animal energy and if no vestige of a flock remains, The Lambs are no less a necessary

Bach and Saint-Saëns. Having outlived a normal long Karakul lifetime by 50 percent, Bach and Saint-Saëns were as beautiful and distinguished as ever. Although I understood that flocking animals were known to be happier in a group of at least four, I made the decision that this was their home and that we ought to live out their lives together. When there were just the two of them, it was increasingly difficult for me to leave them, and but for a few absences, I was at the farm with them all of that final year. It was a precious time, and nothing was more important to me than to be with Saint-Saëns and Bach, who had shared with me these truly blessed years, surrounded by the natural loveliness of the countryside and bonded by the eloquent silent vocabulary with which we communicated.

presence in the landscape. We are extensions of one another, true companions. It is the noon peace, when the shepherds of the ancient pastoral verse rest in the shade among their flocks to compose their songs. I enjoy a complete solidarity with Le Berceau and Saint-Saëns and Bach. This is everything.

Bach and Saint-Saëns might have been willing to resume our morning walks along the stream. They had, without invitation, followed me to the gateposts shortly after Poulenc's burial.

I am now the one who is shy of the morning circuit and cannot allow myself to forget that incident at the pond when the poor lost beagle sent them running in all directions. There are more dogs in the area now. What if I were out in the front pasture with two elderly sheep when a couple of dogs ambled across the property? I will never know because I do not accept the risk. And so our days are spent up around the barn or the house, or under the old oak tree that shades the terrace.

59

Tea Parties

Summer is here in its full glory. It is one of those early afternoons that sometimes appear at the beginning of July, fresh, rested hours in which joyful and unexpected events seem possible. Saint-Saëns and Bach and I pass the time on an old faded rose-colored taffeta quilt under the oak tree. I never open my book. My strawberries were for Saint-Saëns, apparently. I lie on my back and look into the solid green of the oak leaves above.

Bach lies on my left. He stretches out his front leg, lays his lovely beige head on it, and falls asleep. His soft snores add to the background ripple of the water below us and the continuous twitter of the birds above. Saint-Saëns is busy inspecting first the disappointing plate on which he has left not a single strawberry and then my book, which remains closed and therefore intact.

Then he settles to my right. His heavy tail flops slightly to the side, revealing the color of black pearls on its smooth fleshy underside. I stretch out my left arm and Saint-Saëns rests his head on it. He, too, becomes still and perhaps intermittently dozes between long periods of watching me and restfully chewing a pulverized mass of grasses and clover and strawberries.

Not all of our afternoons are spent lying on an old quilt under the oak tree. Often at the weekend, one or two friends come for tea. Today our guest is a lovely Englishwoman. I've placed a small table under the tree. Bach and Saint-Saëns sniff around it for any hint of what is to come. As I arrange wicker chairs for the lady and me, suspense builds. The Lambs vacuum up the sides and backs of the chairs.

My guest understands that The Lambs will join us. She has survived countless luncheons at the Big Table. On more than one occasion, Ginastera tipped her out of her chair as he emerged from underneath it, blindfolded by the tablecloth. Today, tea and anchovy sandwiches are safe. Bach folds down at one end of the table, Saint-Saëns at my side, and, shaded by wide-brimmed straw hats, my guest and I are able to converse about her childhood in India and the condition of her roses.

The table under the tree becomes a regular feature of our lazy summer afternoons. There can be no fresh fruit or cucumber sandwiches, but Bach and Saint-Saëns decline cakes and even frosted sugar cookies. I can almost hear them saying, *No gingersnaps? This place is getting dull!*

60

Late Nights

On these long warm afternoons, the time of retiring to the barn for the night stretches further and further toward darkness. The shadow of the old oak tree reaches down the slope, and The Lambs follow it to nip grass almost to the side of the barn. Seeing them at that end of the lawn, I assume they are ready to settle in for the night.

Wrong. They follow me onto the front step of the barn. Then Bach darts back up the slope. Saint-Saëns follows. Tonight I am fortunate, and with a bribe of a few gingersnaps, they dutifully shamble in. Some evenings are not entertaining. I may sit in the office for an hour or more, hoping they'll give up and wander in. Other nights, I go up to the loft and sort books for a while before trying once again to coax them in.

I know what the problem is. They know that as soon as I close the doors, I will desert them. I can picture the outline of their two heads—Bach's neck gaunt with age—as they lie in the run-in, look-ing out past the despised fence into the distance, two lonely old sheep, all alone for yet another night.

Gradually, I extend my time with them until the sky is filled with stars. I enjoy these hours of their quiet companionship. As much as the bustle of the larger group amused me, it is the silent company of Bach and Saint-Saëns during these long summer days that will come back to me, so intense is the sanctuary I share with them.

Under the red oak tree. The months with only Saint-Saëns and Bach were a time of unspeakable peace and tranquillity. We took no long walks around the perimeter of the property. Instead, we lounged around close to one of the buildings. On most afternoons, we installed ourselves under the old oak tree that protected the back of the house. It was risky to read, as Saint-Saëns had developed a taste for pages of books. But just to have their gentle company for hours meant everything to me. It is here that we spent the fabled August night that was too atrociously hot for them to survive the barn.

61

Slumber Party

Out of nowhere, the second week of August blasts forth. It grinds its fist down on us as the temperatures sizzle at one hundred degrees before noon. Joshua quickly installs the window fans. The Lambs are good sports. Bach positions himself in the cooled air from one fan while Saint-Saëns twists his back to get the full value of the other. In the late afternoon, I turn them off. All they're doing is moving hot air around. I resume my practice of washing The Lambs' faces with cold water and pressing ice cubes down through their fleeces.

Then comes the tenth of August. My neighbor arrives in the middle of the afternoon with a supply of two-gallon containers of water. He warns that it's time to prepare for a serious drought. The village bank sign reports a temperature of 108 degrees. The air does not move.

At nine o'clock in the evening, the sky is a dusky mud. The Lambs, sprawled on the grass under the oak tree, do not move as I walk down to the barn. I step in. It is a furnace. There is no way that I am going to force them into this building tonight. We will simply stay together up at the house. Maybe the air up there will move during the night.

I light all the candles in the sconces on the terrace. The Lambs watch me intently. *Isn't it time to go in? Hasn't she been complaining about maneuvering us into the barn? Tonight must be a party!*

It is. Extravagantly wasting cooled air, I open the first-floor windows as wide as possible to let Mozart flute quartets billow out onto our caravanserai. I place a large pan of cold water on the ground for The Lambs and pour a glass of chilled sauvignon blanc for myself. Eventually, black darkness settles over us. There is not a single star. And absolutely no reprieve from the heat. The Lambs arrange themselves at opposite ends of the quilt, leaving the center to me. We do, surprisingly, manage to sleep. I know this because Bach wakes me in the early morning when he begins to shift his body. We wait quietly until Saint-Saëns responds to the first hint of dawn, rousing himself in air that is as hot as it was last night.

As August stretches out, there are no more nights like the tenth. There is no more scorchingly hot weather. Now there are comfortable daily lunches on the terrace with Bach and Saint-Saëns. Together, we watch the leaves turn from green to gold and rust. It will not be long until the dogwoods flicker into red. The warm afternoons on the grass under the oak tree ease into days when a sweater is welcome. It is time to schedule a visit from the shearer. Like old humans, Bach and Saint-Saëns produce far less wool now, roughly half the amount that fall shearing would have produced even five years ago.

Tea parties under the tree have gained in popularity, and gradually a few interesting cocktails find their way into our repertoire. Saint-Saëns is not shy about lifting the orange slices and celery out of our experiments with Pimm's.

One afternoon, a former client joins this happy scene. He was with one of the major Swiss banks and has great business sense. "You ought to be cashing out of here, you know," he tells me. "The place is beautiful. You're right on the edge of the Virginia hunt country and all that. But it looks like the housing bubble will burst in Australia, then the UK, and then here."

"Yes, I'm aware of that," I reply. "But this is the home of two elderly sheep. They are not going anywhere. And neither am I, for as long as they are here."

62

Winter

As the days pick up the tingling chill of fall, my neighbor arrives with our supply of fragrant fresh orchardgrass to store in the loft. On his next trip, he delivers a load of straw for me to furnish the run-in. If summer has been gentle, winter is predicted to be almost an extension of it. The word from the village barbershop is that the farmers are not talking about the usual February ice storms but are worrying about the water supply for next year.

I barely notice that it is officially winter and time to decamp to the straw salon. For now, I spend my afternoons with The Lambs in the barn. Even though we have our electrified waterer in the run-in, I still keep plastic buckets of water for them inside the barn. I fill them in the mornings while they eat. I notice that the water in one bucket is very low by noon. Where is all this water going? I wonder. There is no leak, no water on the floor. Mysterious. Half a bucket of water gone in the two hours we've been in the barn. I watch.

It doesn't take long to see that Saint-Saëns is spending more and more time sucking water out of that bucket.

"Dr. Comyn, is the excessive drinking of water of any concern to you?"

"What do you mean by 'excessive'?"

"Gallons." I note that he seems to hesitate before replying.

"Well, that in itself doesn't really tell me anything. I wouldn't worry about it, but I'd sure keep an eye on it."

There is talk of my father's return in the springtime. A friend in Montana has offered to escort him across the country on the train. I research the train schedules, but I can't pretend that he's able to make another trip. I suggest to him that we keep in touch by telephone. We agree that a call at 3:30 my time would suit both of us.

For a couple of weeks, I have to be careful to leave lunches in the village in time for my daily call, but the regular conversation quickly becomes an important part of my days. He tells me that he is able to translate stories from the Greek. He often mentions his progress with the black leather journal. He has decided to give away his car.

I do not dwell on the subject of the future of The Lambs. We know exactly what we will do at the appropriate time. All hearts and minds—Dr. Comyn's, Joshua's, and mine—all agree that we are comfortable with our strategy for the final moment. No further questions to resolve, I sink deeper and deeper into the woolly presence of The Lambs, and each day is a day of thanksgiving for the time that I have here with them.

63

A Long Way

Suddenly, it is Thursday in the first week of April, not yet convincingly springtime, but Washington is a palette of greens, with crocuses and daffodils peeking out of lawns. I am making one of my rare trips into the city, and this morning I luxuriate in the company of my piano teacher, who delights me with his latest Poulenc discovery. He has an extra copy of this gorgeous piece, the "XIIIème Improvisation," and I carry it home as though it were a valuable painting.

As always, the minute I return to Le Berceau, I go into the barn. No one greets me at the door with a mischievous head butt. Saint-Saëns stands in the center of the floor. His eyes are wild, feverish. He throws his head over his shoulder and flies off into the paddock. Bach, dazed by all this ferocity, turns to watch Saint-Saëns charge around in circles. I step into the office. Joshua sits with his chin in his hand.

"I know," he says. "It happened to me when I came in to feed this morning. I've already called Dr. Comyn."

"And?"

"He ought to be here any minute now. He wanted to be sure you were home."

Before there is time to speculate on Saint-Saëns, Dr. Comyn enters the barn. There are no pleasantries.

"I wasn't far away, and I know how you feel about this. I didn't really want to tell you on the phone, but something like this is what I've been watching for. I mean, the excessive drinking, well, that can be a few different things. It also seemed to me he might be gaining weight. But a drastic personality change like this means there has to be a tumor somewhere on his brain. The water intake and a weight gain would suggest a pituitary adenoma. We'll have to take care of this immediately."

"What do you mean 'immediately'?" I ask, knowing what the answer will be: "I'll be here before seven in the morning."

Joshua says, "Miss George, if you don't mind, I'd like to make the trip to the funeral home tomorrow by myself."

Friday. The uncertain gray of dawn. I step into the barn. Bach and Saint-Saëns are standing by the hayracks on the opposite wall. No one comes to greet me, but no one wildly takes flight. I walk past them into the run-in. The air is grisaille and brittle as glass. Reduced to bare necessities. Gone is all the soft opiate frivolity of the countryside, all the fragrance of aromatic pastures.

Bach. Noble Bach, who from his first day on earth maintained this stately posture. After Ginastera died, Bach might have assumed the leadership role. He was willing, on the first trip into the forest without Ginastera, to lead the group, but only so far; then they all reversed their direction and hastened back to the barn. We all knew that Bach had developed a strong attachment to Joshua, and it seemed at times that Dr. Comyn had a special place in his heart for him. This was confirmed on the day we had a celebration to honor the one-year anniversary of the deaths of the final two lambs. It was a perfect gray early-April day, complete with rain dripping into our champagne. No one was surprised that Dr. Comyn walked over to Bach's grave and said, "He was my favorite."

In the run-in, the straw bales of my winter furniture lend the only color to the picture, a harsh greenish gray yellow. The Lambs do not run from me, but I sense their uneasiness. None of the usual sniffing around the feed troughs. Bach watches me closely as I sit down on a straw bale. Saint-Saëns approaches. I am grateful for this time alone with them. I turn first toward Saint-Saëns and then to Bach. I cannot stop looking at them.

Joshua drives in, slowly for once, perhaps out of reverence or to capture the scene for the last time. He enters the barn and stands against the run-in doorjamb. Later I will learn that he had come in during the night "to give them one last gingersnap and say good-bye." We exchange no words. Everything we will need this morning is laid out on a bench, two of my favorite white wool blankets, red twine from hay bales.

Dr. Comyn arrives.

Now I hear the crack of folding doors. Slide bolts shoved into the floor. Dr. Comyn gently steers Bach into the hall beside the office. Saint-Saëns and I move into the interior and wait beside the east wall. I rest my palms on his back. My legs press against his left side. Doors creak open.

Dr. Comyn comes to kneel in front of Saint-Saëns. Joshua stations himself at his tail. Dr. Comyn finds the right jugular vein and injects the barbiturate. Saint-Saëns takes one slight step back into Joshua's embrace.

And now I am walking slowly behind Joshua's pickup, which carries the last two lambs, wrapped in white wool blankets. As he turns to go up the lane, I walk back to the barn as though I'm asleep. I enter. I go to the place where I stood beside Saint-Saëns. The impression of his body is still in the sawdust. I kneel, and then I lie down inside his outline, extending my arms where his front legs lay. I inhale the perfume of the fresh pine sawdust.

All this is a long way from the Karakul bazaar of Bokhara. The shepherds of Arcadia are farther away still, early milestones on a flowery path that meanders through the scenery of Wordsworth and Poussin. Any lingering anxieties about the lamb on prehistoric man's altar are diffused in the dark, hollow chamber that once resonated with music and laughter and scuffling and the munching of hay.

I never again sit on the grass under the old oak tree. That is where Saint-Saëns sat.

The Lambs have been lifted out of my reach by the gleaming spiral that delivered them. But still they are here, inside me and all around me. I understand how we must lose our earthly paradise in order actually to live in it, to experience it in the reality of its images. Now it is truly mine to repossess in the invisible world of my imagination, in "poetry country," the most real of all worlds.

As I had known all along, that wonderful long summer was my father's last visit to Le Berceau. Now almost every other month, I travel out to Montana to visit him and to hold his dear old hands. Only two years after I buried Bach and Saint-Saëns, and as soon as the heavy snows of February receded, I telephoned him. "Daddy, how would you like a visit?"

"Oh, honey, not now. Why don't you wait until the weather is better?"

On the following Monday, I went. The friend who met me at the airport asked, "How do you feel after traveling all day?"

"I feel fine," I replied.

"Good. We're going to the hospital." My friend has been very close to my father since she and I were in high school together. She doesn't have to explain anything.

There he sat in a gorgeous red silk dressing gown, surrounded by dozens of red roses. Of course he was delighted by my surprise appearance, but when I arrived, he was busy entertaining his visitors with a story about a taxi ride through rural Greece. Before I left that evening, he asked me to bring him a supply of good red wine when I come back the next day.

We shared some splendid hours with the attorney who had been at Le Berceau with us, reminiscing about the antics of Ginastera and Poulenc, and comparing notes on how many things Saint-Saëns had chewed.

One afternoon, just the two of us were together for more than three hours. There were no intrusions by hospital staff. We simply were in each other's presence. We had arrived in that exquisite place where words were unnecessary. At one point, he recited Wordsworth's Immortality Ode in its entirety.

Eventually, the spell was broken by a man who came in to dust the floor. As soon as he left, we said the Lord's Prayer together. And then I kissed him on his forehead and said I'd be back in the morning.

When I telephoned the hospital at eight o'clock the next day, I was told that he had "slipped away" just a few minutes earlier. A life of ninety-eight years had ended with as much composure as it had been lived.

As soon as I returned to the farm, my neighbor and I unfurled a length of rich black English wool that was stretched out on a pole across the highest rafters of the barn. Majestically draping to the floor, it was like a stone stela rising from a clearing in the heart of a forest, a fabric monument to solemnly absorb the sentiments of friends, some of whom traveled considerable distances to honor a rare combination of intelligence and kindness. Six weeks later, with quiet devotion and decorum, several kindred spirits and I placed the hat of Rameau's wool—inside which was a portion of my father's ashes—beneath the rose planted on top of Satie's remains.

When it was time to bury Rameau, I had been drawn to this place on the high ground, where earth meets heaven, where all dream sheep ascend to live among the stars. All of The Lambs and now my father are buried here, in a tight cluster of grave markers, protected by eight very old tulip-poplars. These trees are so evenly spaced, they appear to have been planted in this formation. How wonderful it would be, I think, for something to be climbing up their tall, straight trunks.

All I can think of now is the idea of rose blooms covering these trees. Living beauty to shelter the cemetery. A few afternoons with my rose books, and I order one hundred bare-root plants of Mademoiselle Cécile Brünner, which can thrive without all-day direct sunlight and will produce dark green foliage, pale pink blossoms, and the unmistakable fragrance of old French roses.

My neighbors are delighted to have a happy project here again. I figure out the spacing of the roses around the trees. The ground is damp, and it takes no time to prepare the holes. We crawl around on our hands and knees to position the plants. There is plenty of talk about what The Lambs would have done to fresh rosebuds.

Soon there will be new life on this treasured ground. Since old roses do not produce blooms in the first year, there is the promise of their mellifluous perfume next spring.

64

Poetry Country

I have known all along that "poetry country" is a landscape of the mind. It is the interior country of the imagination, where streams and meadows and stars, sun and moon, trees and birds and lambs, exist not only as natural objects but as imaginative experiences, as well. Similarly, in this country, the inhabitants are spiritual beings as well as material.

Poetry country is the deepest and highest place of the mind. It is the truth of myself as well as the means through which I can recognize the truth of the other, the land, the lamb, you. I never planned, never strived to come to this place. All I did was consent to the inner promptings of my soul. It was the urging of my soul that established me here in my rightful place, where I could learn to be receptive to the living creative impulse within me.

As The Lambs made their gentle spiral up into their next greensward and as my father wrote his last lines in the black leather journal, I did not cling to them. I knew they were all gifts. I had only to accept them and hold them tenderly, until the appointed time to commend them back to the place from which they had come, and then to continue to braid their spirits into the rope that is my life.

My thoughts turn to Le Berceau. The barn is empty. My father's rooms. One afternoon, I am standing upstairs. I look out the window to the pasture below. And there I see my father, with his old wool hat and his hawthorn walking stick, surrounded by a group of lambs, walking in the usual direction. The emotion that I have held inside me for months floods out. I think of my father's last view of Le Berceau, The Lambs and me standing at the gates. It is time to have the final stanza of Walter de la Mare's "Fare Well" engraved onto a brass plate to attach to the old green bench at the pond. That old bench—so lovingly chewed and patched and rubbed all these years—has been a daily reminder of our dedication to the sacred realm of the poetic imagination. These were some of my father's favorite lines:

> *Look thy last on all things lovely,*
> *Every hour. Let no night*
> *Seal thy sense in deathly slumber*
> > *Till to delight*
> *Thou have paid thy utmost blessing;*
> *Since that all things thou wouldst praise*
> *Beauty took from those who loved them*
> > *In other days.*

65

Path

In her second year, Mademoiselle Cécile Brünner created a room of her fragrance around her, even before the buds popped open. I didn't think of it immediately, but as the canes stretched out, I was delighted by the idea of wrapping them around the trees in parallel helixes. This ancient symbol, held in place with dark green hemp twine, honors the upward spiral of the sheep.

It has been a long time since I walked the path that The Lambs and I trod every day. There were times when I was tempted to retrace the circuit, but either the grass was too high or the heat too oppressive. Today is ideal, and I am eager to make the journey. I won't be alone. This is something to be done in the company of the spirits who made the trip with me in the past.

The gates are locked. It is a triumphant August day. Blue sky, a few enormous clouds, a slight tingle of chill unusual in Virginia at this time of the year. The kind of day that would send Ginastera springing into the air and propel Saint-Saëns and Mozart onto their rear legs to nip maple leaves. I will push open the front doors of the barn at exactly half past eight, the moment Ginastera would have been positioned, ready to lead his troupe.

The barn is still throbbing from a recent party. All swept out and polished, it had been waiting for something, as had my local friends. My piano tuner knew of a chamber group coming to Charlottesville. Perfect. A dinner below and musicians in the loft, waves of Debussy and Ravel. Fauré and some Vivaldi. All serene and lovely until someone popped a guitar out of a case and an accordion appeared. Suddenly, I was hearing tango, and I will never forget when the strings lashed into the most amazing piece of symphonic music I've ever heard. Afterward, I asked the director what it was. He said it was "Libertango," by Astor Piazzolla, who had been a student of one of the greats of the southern hemisphere. Maybe I'd heard of him. Alberto Ginastera.

This morning, I'm early and could sit in the barn and sip tea from a pretty porcelain cup without concern of Saint-Saëns's nose in it. But I can't wait another minute. Like a pagan gaily returning to his sylvan deities, I bound up the road toward the forest. I can feel Ginastera's pulsating Latin energy urging me forward, and I have to move along to keep up with my flock.

I step onto the path that The Lambs laid out so well. Shoulder-high dogwood branches brush against me as I proceed into the depth of the wood. Someone has hollowed out the top section of the poetry bench, but it's sturdy enough for me to sit for a few minutes. I would open the rusted candy tin and read a cherished poem, but a deer has stepped on it, and the pages inside are scraps. Anyway, I am being pulled forward by my invisible companions.

We leave the forest and spill out into the flat front pasture. I automatically feel Debussy's snout slide into the palm of my left hand. The grass is only as high as my knees, and I can walk directly to the corner where our trail begins. I can't wait to see if I can find the path, which was eventually an actual furrow that could have been dug out with a shovel.

Across the front, the dawn redwoods have grown at least forty feet tall. In time, they will be twice that, but even now they form a convincing wall. About ten years ago, I named these trees for kings and queens of France who had in some way advanced the French landscape tradition. Empress Josephine, who so courageously survived her ordeals and amassed her famous collection of roses, stands next to the gates. To her left is Louis XIV, whose garden contribution is legendary. Left of him is Louis XIII, during whose reign the flower-embroidered parterres reached their pinnacle. Farther left is King Henri IV, whose second wife, Marie de' Medici, brought to France her great love of the Italian landscape tradition.

I am standing in the far corner, directly in front of Queen Eleanor of Aquitaine, who is covered with new growth at her tips. She occupies this signal position not because of any specific garden association, but because she is my role model. Imagine this. She was imprisoned by her husband for sixteen years. Whether she was guilty or innocent of his charges is irrelevant. What matters to me is that she emerged from her confinement more powerful than ever, with no apparent reduction in energy, dignity, or vision. According to the chroniclers, throughout the entire time, she was arrayed in her shimmering satin gowns trimmed in ermine, and she always stood tall and regal despite what must have been trying circumstances. I think about her almost every day.

Ginastera also thought about her every day. The moment we arrived in this corner, he rushed at her for a mouthful of turpentine-flavored needles. (Yes, I know how they taste.) And had I not been there to steer him onto the path, Bach would have joined the assault. Today it feels as if she knows I am here for an important purpose. She silently greets me with her characteristic aplomb.

Now I turn to the stream and begin my walk where I imagine the old path was. The grasses are as tall as I am, and there is not so much as a hint of our route. Large low-slung sheep bodies and many hooves were necessary to maintain it. Without the path in front of me, I look at everything as if I've never seen it before. There are vivid lime green grasses that I don't recognize. I do not recall shoulder-high wild daisies.

As I progress along the path, I am reminded of the overwhelming sense of security I feel in this place, so tenderly am I surrounded by the spirit of all that is here and the spirits of all who are no longer here. I arrive at the Big Table. The gold chairs have survived the floods, but they've been mended so often, they look like Lego log constructions. I sit under the sycamore trees, looking toward the pond while The Lambs spread out to search for patches of orchardgrass.

How beautiful they are as they perform their naturally assigned task of cleaning the surface of the earth and converting the vegetation into nutrients and wool. The merry meals shared here are unforgettable, but so, too, are the mornings I spent with Plato and Bergson and Mary Midgley. Soon Ginastera will dive under the table to scratch his back, and Saint-Saëns will come for a nip of my new leather shoelaces.

Sitting here, soaking in the atmosphere, I can feel the poetry and music and prayer that infuse this place. I step over to the stream. It is gleaming through the tree trunks. It is the most beautiful water in the world. Pinpoints of sunlight catch the ripples, and it seems that sprites are dancing on its surface. It has never been more musical than it is today with its clinking melody that might be heard in a garden in Kyoto.

As I leave the table, my heart is going out to every tree along the stream and to every tree at the edge of the forest across the pasture. I have the distinct feeling that they are reaching back to me. I wave to Pan and return to the path. How my father would have loved this expedition!

Now the path turns at the end of the field and will take me back along the other side of the property. I stop to smile at the enormous granite rock on the other side of the stream. Those were the days! My father and I waded over to lunch there. We often lingered for hours, discussing new ideas or sharing old times. Certainly a bottle of wine. One of us would invariably fall in the water on the return crossing.

What a wonderful sport he was. When I was young, I took it for granted that all men were as honest as he was and had hearts as great and faithful as his. I had much to learn.

I am now opposite the barn and the site of the dreadful security pen. After passing by several huge maples, I reach the first of the ten stone steps. I follow them as they curve up from the lower level of pasture. When I reach the high ground, I can see down the entire length of the fields below me. It brings to my mind the view that propelled my father and me off in search of The Lambs. Today, though, I am not imagining a pastoral scene with the required stage properties of a stream and shade trees, a flowery meadow, and, of course, a little flock of sheep. That scene is permanently embedded inside me.

The stream tinkles below, and birdsong floats over from the forest. While I am standing here, it seems that the air becomes lighter and the light becomes brighter. I feel energized and lifted. Just behind me is the marvel of the rose-wrapped tulip-poplars. Dozens of late blooms send their antique fragrance in my direction. I turn to walk over to the graves that lie at the feet of these old trees. I know I am on sacred ground, and I wonder if I ought to remove my shoes.

I remember that afternoon when I lay on the ground while all of The Lambs grazed, and how, after a time, they came over and arranged themselves around me, so that by slightly turning my head, I saw only black legs, and then white legs and beige legs, slowly rotating. It was in that embrace that I claimed my gift of writing.

So many precious moments like that are collected here in this place. I cannot leave. But simply to stand here seems inadequate, and like that day of the encasing legs, I slowly sink to the ground, lie on my back, and stretch out my arms. There are no sheep legs to form a wall around me. Today my eyes follow the nearest rose-draped tulip-poplar to its tip, where it meets the sea blue sky.

The sky is completely clear except for one large cloud. It is not

Trees at cemetery. The pets' cemetery lies inside a semicircular formation of eight enormous old tulip-poplars, so perfectly spaced in this configuration that their planting appears to have been intentional. Several years after all thirteen lambs had died, I felt that it would be good to add something beautiful and luxuriantly growing to this area. It had to be roses. So we spaced one hundred climbing plants of Mademoiselle Cécile Brünner, a lovely old French rose, around the bases of the trees. No blooms came in the first year, but the canes stretched out beautifully. We wound them around and up the trunks of the trees, securing them with dark green hemp twine. By the second year, the canes had climbed so high that we needed our tallest ladders to tie them in. Only later on did I register that by creating these spirals of roses up the trees, we had reinterpreted the spiral of dream sheep that had forecast the arrival of The Lambs into my mind and into my world. At first, it seemed as though this was nothing more than a coincidence, but I know it was not.

moving. After a while, an air current pushes it slightly forward. When this happens, a small fleecy ball breaks off at the front corner. I am instantly reminded of Charpentier's practice of leaving the group to graze by himself at the far end of the pasture. The air changes again. A piece comes loose at the other end. Surely this is Debussy coming to rest her chin in my hand. Now the cloud breaks again, and in the front three small ovals take shape: Ginastera, Bach, and Saint-Saëns.

The clouds are an incandescent white, and yet I can smell Debussy's vaguely almond scent. Saint-Saëns's wool carried a richer burnt sugar fragrance, and I can smell it now, too. I have often thought that even if I were blindfolded I would be able to distinguish the texture and the scent of each lamb's fleece.

And now, tenderly, the air gathers all the pieces back into one large oval. It begins to move away. No. Wait, I want to say. Don't go yet. But The Lambs are living in an order outside time. I know where they are. Sometimes they appear in the music of their namesakes, so real that I can reach out and feel the warmth of a body. At other times, especially on warm afternoons, they come to me on a wave of lanolin.

Today they exist in a pure white silhouette suspended in the deep blue heavens. Pure white in the deep blue beyond. Floating above, bearing light.

Afterword

It has been said that *memory* and *imagination* are convertible terms, and while *The Lambs* is a memoir, it is also a product of my memory.

In writing this story, my model was "The little shepherd" from Claude Debussy's *Children's Corner*. Striving toward that purity and clarity of line, I occasionally rearranged events. I reduced most of the characters to ciphers. Others, who might reasonably have appeared, were suppressed entirely.

So, rather than pinpointing its genre, perhaps it is preferable to consider this book simply as a work of art. For art always involves a process of selection.

Acknowledgments

Over the past dozen years, I have received so much help from so many people that I am humbled by such generosity. They have made the research and writing of this story a very rich experience by sharing their expert knowledge, reading chapters or entire early unedited versions, opening address books, and answering my many and repeated questions. They have all been true teachers.

I owe a particular debt of gratitude to Philip Glazebrook, whose book *Journey to Khiva* was my first glimpse into Central Asia. We then corresponded for several years—his letters were always filled with lists of books I had to read—and there were many fascinating telephone conversations. He had Karakul-related stories: he told me that on some of his short flights between cities in Uzbekistan it was not unusual to have a few Karakul sheep at the back of the plane. Over tea in London, he urged me to plunge into this fascinating area of the world and to write my story, which would shine an unusual light on its culture.

My first forays into the serious study of Central Asia took me into the treasure trove of the Near East Section of the African and Middle

Eastern Division of the Library of Congress. Dr. Chris Murphy, head of the section, gave me inexhaustible guidance and hospitality. Chris, himself, has remained a loyal ally in addition to generously offering the talents of his staff, especially of Hirad Dinavari and Dr. Anchi Hoh. Over the years he has shared much personal advice and has taken time, more than once, to review sections of the book. His keen-eyed reading of the manuscript led to many corrections. Surely there are still mistakes, but these are solely my responsibility, and not his. Central Asia expert Professor S. Frederick Starr was also kind enough to read the book and offer very welcome suggestions. I will never forget a long conversation over lunch with Rev. Professor David Brown, when he led me into the subject of ritual sacrifice, and I thank Professor Robert Pogue Harrison for his time in long telephone conversations on this subject and the formidable reading list he recommended.

In the library of the National Gallery of Art I had the help of so many people over the years that my list could be infinitely extended. Andrea Gibbs found many visual images that enhanced my appreciation of my subject; Ted Dalziel is that gifted kind of researcher who independently identified books I needed before I knew I needed them. Don Henderson was generous with his experience in book design and the business of selling books.

Dr. Gordon Braden at the University of Virginia and Brandon Maynard at Oxford University Press rescued me when I needed their expert advice urgently. Patrick Kilmer, in the reference department of the Jefferson-Madison Regional Library, has located and borrowed dozens of books from other libraries for me. Without the creativity of Richard Van Nice, my talented book detective in Montana, I would never have been able to see many obscure old books that gave such texture to the journey into Central Asia.

Anneke Jakes of The Livestock Conservancy gave me the starting point for my research into the history of the Karakul sheep; Dr. Alison Martin and Ryan Walker have been faithful supporters throughout the project. Richard Fabrizio, at J. Mendel in New York, taught me the intricacies of using the lambskins and shared his fur industry library with me. My Persian friend, Roz Farhadi, always stopped whatever he was doing to tell me about Persian poets or foods or customs.

When I began the actual writing, I relied heavily on the people who are characters in the story. My contractor, Joseph Wayner, answered endless questions about building details. Joshua Clemons kindly read several sections. My county extension agent, Brad Jarvis, who continues to be very important to every phase of this book's existence, read several drafts of the manuscript. My loyal neighbor, Scott Evans, was steadfast through the entire experience. It was to him that I turned for verification of anything related to leaves and trees. I am deeply grateful to Dr. Patrick Comyn, who read several versions of the manuscript and stayed with me to the very end to help smooth out some of the dialogue. My piano teacher in Washington, Dr. Charles Timbrell, generously checked and rechecked the references to music. Sadly, two faithful neighbors, Robert Dorsey and Pete Clark, did not live to see the completed summary of our wonderful shared adventure.

The man with the Cambodian *khloy* in his pocket is Ambassador Sichan Siv, who was with us on numerous memorable occasions, several of which were anniversaries of important successes of his. His entire life is a success story, recounted in his magisterial memoir,

Golden Bones, which traces his career from his escape from the killing fields of the Khmer Rouge to his appointment as the American representative to the United Nations Economic and Social Council. The law professor I mention is Dr. Ved Nanda at the University of Denver. His influence on me is lifelong, and there is no way to adequately express my gratitude to him for his abiding inspiration and encouragement. Of course, my dear and departed parents were deeply interested in this project. My father would have relished reliving the years recorded in the narrative, and my mother's last words to me were a benediction on my new writing career.

As a book began to emerge from all its multiple strands, a few absolutely devoted friends were willing to read early drafts. It is hard to imagine. John Berger read several of these and made encouraging comments. Tracy Brown, Martha Patillo Siv, Harry Eyres, Philip Tedeschi, Genevieve Overy, Father Jeremiah Sullivan, Carole Thompson, Father Laurence Freeman, Michael Brophy, and Roy Howat also read those very long early versions, more than once, and encouraged me to keep working.

Gene Baur, founder of Farm Sanctuary, has followed the development of my story since I began writing it. He has read numerous versions and opened some important doors for me. More recently I have worked with Sylvia Moskovitz of his staff, and she is simply visionary. It is my pleasure to donate a portion of the proceeds from the sale of this book to Farm Sanctuary.

Other dear friends made many excellent suggestions, opened doors, and offered perpetual encouragement, and I thank them very sincerely: Libby d'Hémery, Mary Weinmann, John Diquollo, Alexandra de Borchgrave, Professor Reuben Rainey, Linda Robinson, Margitta

Muhlenberg, Michael Richwine, David Marshall, Slaviśa Milanović, Elizabeth Barlow Rogers, Betsy Shortell, Susan Cohen, Elena Son, John Brademas's entire staff, Lenette Crescimanno, Lee Gildea, and Carol Troxell. Cyril Harris got in the last word.

When I met legendary editor Chuck Adams at a book festival, the real life of this book began. He generously read an early version and told me to take out about half of it. He then referred me to an independent editor. This advice led to one of the finest experiences of the project. Over the course of the past five years, Kenny Marotta has been supremely generous with his wisdom and experience. Not only did he guide me into shaping a book out of a pile of pages, he also generously taught me a course in creative writing and supported me in a way that was not only inspiring but life-enhancing. Down to searching out a needed quote at the very end, he was essential to this book, and I am forever grateful to him. This is not to suggest that Chuck Adams abandoned me. He has made additional suggestions on numerous aspects of the project all along the way, and his sharp eye and unswerving backing were as reliable as they were invaluable. I have unlimited thanks for his good counsel.

Daniel Hallahan has been a pillar of support for years. Not only has he read numerous versions of the manuscript and made helpful suggestions, but without his constant good humor and talent with all things related to the technology involved, I would not have survived. Dani Antol, Fonda Hill, and Cheryl Brown patiently sorted and catalogued hundreds of images of sheep. Scott Cook applied all of his skill to making the best of the photographs, and working with him was always a complete joy. John James drew the beautiful map of the property.

My friend Jon Sweeney, together with the indomitable Phyllis Tickle, introduced me to my literary agent, Kathleen Davis Niendorff, who, with creativity, enthusiasm and skill, safely delivered *The Lambs* and me to St. Martin's Press/Thomas Dunne Books and proved to be a highly skilled and loyal counselor during the production process. Thanks are due to the entire production team of St. Martin's Press. Marcia Markland, project editor, certainly demonstrated her skills in coordinating every step; her editorial assistant, Nettie Finn, was always charming; and to have David Stanford Burr, published poet, as production editor for a story set in "poetry country" was almost too good to be true. My sincere thanks go to my copyeditor, Carol Edwards, whose humanity, knowledge and love of literature, and refined sensibility, irradiated every page she touched. I was blessed to have my trusted and longtime friend Harry Jaffe, acclaimed journalist and author, as my mentor and guide during the final phases of the project.

My own faithful assistant, Karin Merrill, was a true companion on this journey. She saw every single early attempt and accompanied me through it all with honesty, cleverness, and never-failing encouragement. Her warm and steadying presence in the project was absolutely essential, and I will never forget the experiences we shared along the way.

Very special gratitude goes to my most perceptive friend, Alasdair Forbes, who accompanied me poetically and intellectually on this rich journey into a cherished chapter of my life. When I was approaching the end of the writing, he insisted upon reviewing it, although it was a very busy time for him. His reading was deep and penetrating, and his characteristic acuity, sensitivity, and vision produced several single-spaced pages of improvements. I consider those pages the true measure of friendship, and they will always be precious to me.

A guardian angel was assigned to this project in the form of Dr. Mary Midgley. Long before I thought of writing a book about my sheep, I had read and reread her many books about animals and their importance to us. Before I even had an outline, she generously spent several wonderful hours over lunch with me in London. Later, the time we shared in her home, quietly discussing our topic, gave a profound and unforgettable richness to the experience. She has read every version of this book over the years and has given me many ideas and much encouragement. Mostly I treasure her inspiration and her commitment to her own pursuit of excellence. It is a privilege to dedicate this book to her.

Bibliography

BOOKS

ANIMALS

Baker, J. A. *The Peregrine*. New York: New York Review of Books Classics, 1967.

Bekoff, Marc. *The Emotional Lives of Animals*. Novato, California: New World Library, 2007.

Boakes, Robert. *From Darwin to Behaviourism: Psychology and the Minds of Animals*. Cambridge: Cambridge University Press, 1984, digitally printed 2008 version.

Bright, Michael. *Beasts of the Field: The Revealing Natural History of Animals in the Bible*. London: Robson Books, 2006.

Clark, Stephen R. L. *The Moral Status of Animals*. Oxford: Oxford University Press, 1977.

Darwin, Charles. *The Expression of the Emotions in Man and Animals*. 1872. Reprint, Chicago: University of Chicago Press, 1965.

Elton, Charles S. *The Pattern of Animal Communities*. 1966. Reprint, London: Methuen, 1970.

Geist, Valerius. *Mountain Sheep: A Study in Behavior and Evolution*. Chicago: University of Chicago Press, 1971.

Gould, Stephen Jay. *Ever Since Darwin, Reflections in Natural History*. 1977. Reprint, New York: W. W. Norton, 1977.

Lorenz, Konrad. *King Solomon's Ring: New Light on Animal Ways*. 1949. Reprint, London: Routledge, 2002.

——. *On Aggression*. 1963. Reprint, New York: MJF Books, 1966.

Lydekker, Richard. *The Sheep and Its Cousins*. London: George Allen, 1912.

Passmore, John. *Man's Responsibility for Nature: Ecological Problems and Western Traditions*. New York: Charles Scribner's Sons, 1974.

Rowlands, Mark. *The Philosopher and the Wolf: Lessons from the Wild on Love, Death and Happiness*. London: Granta Books, 2008.

Scully, Matthew. *Dominion: The Power of Man, the Suffering of Animals, and the Call to Mercy*. London: Souvenir Press, 2011.

Sheldrake, Rupert. *Dogs That Know When Their Owners Are Coming Home, and Other Unexplained Powers of Animals*. New York: Three Rivers Press, 1999.

ART HISTORY

Blunt, Anthony. *Nicolas Poussin*. 1967. London: Pallas Athene, 1995.

Brunel, Georges. *Boucher*. Translated by Simon Rees, et al. New York: Vendome Press, 1986.

Freedman, Luba. *The Classical Pastoral in the Visual Arts*. New York: Peter Lang, 1989.

Raine, Kathleen. *William Blake*. 1970. Reprint, New York: Thames and Hudson, 1996.

Rosenberg, Pierre, and Keith Christiansen, eds. *Poussin and Nature: Arcadian Visions*. New York: Metropolitan Museum of Art, 2008. Published in conjunction with the exhibition Poussin and Nature: Arcadian Visions.

CENTRAL ASIA

Alexander, Christopher Aslan. *A Carpet Ride to Khiva: Seven Years on the Silk Road*. London: Icon Books, 2010.

Axworthy, Michael. *Iran: Empire of the Mind*. London: Penguin Books, 2008.

Barfield, Thomas J. *The Central Asian Arabs of Afghanistan: Pastoral Nomadism in Transition*. Austin: University of Texas Press, 1981.

Boyce, Mary. *Zoroastrians: Their Religious Beliefs and Practices*. London: Routledge & Kegan Paul, 1987.

Cawthorne, Nigel. *Daughter of Heaven: The True Story of the Only Woman to Become Emperor of China*. Oxford: Oneworld Publications, 2007.

Glazebrook, Philip. *Journey to Khiva: A Writer's Search for Central Asia*. New York: Kodansha, 1996.

Holland, Tom. *Persian Fire: The First World Empire and the Battle for the West*. New York: Anchor Books, 2007.

Hopkirk, Peter. *The Great Game: The Struggle for Empire in Central Asia*. New York: Kodansha, 1994.

Krist, Gustav. *Alone Through the Forbidden Land: Journeys in Disguise Through Soviet Central Asia*. Translated by E. O. Lorimer. London: Faber and Faber, 1938.

Kriwaczek, Paul. *In Search of Zarathustra: The First Prophet and the Ideas That Changed the World*. New York: Alfred A. Knopf, 2003.

Lane Fox, Robin. *The Search for Alexander*. Boston: Little, Brown, 1980.

Marozzi, Justin. *Tamerlane: Sword of Islam, Conqueror of the World*. Cambridge: Da Capo Press, 2007.

Metcalfe, Daniel. *Out of Steppe: The Lost Peoples of Central Asia*. London: Hutchinson, 2009.

Thubron, Colin. *Shadow of the Silk Road*. New York: Harper Perennial, 2008.

Vámbéry, Arminius. *Travels in Central Asia*. London: John Murray, 1864.

Verestchagin, Vassili. *Autobiographical Sketches*. Translated by F. H. Peters. London: Richard Bentley & Son, 1887.

Wood, Frances. *The Silk Road*. Berkeley: University of California Press, 2002.

LITERATURE

Ferdowsi, Abolqasem. *Shahnameh, The Persian Book of Kings*. Translated by Dick Davis. New York: Penguin Books, 2007.

Firdausi. *The Sháh Námeh*. Translated and abridged in prose and verse by James Atkinson, Esq., and edited by Rev. J. A. Atkinson. London: Frederick Warne, 1886.

Herodotus. *The Histories*. Translated by A. D. Godley. 1921. Reprint, Cambridge: Harvard University Press, 1957.

Longus. *Daphnis and Chloe*. Translated by Ronald McCail. Oxford: Oxford University Press, 2009.

Virgil. *Aeneid*. Translated by Robert Fagles. New York: Penguin Books, 2008.

PASTORAL LITERATURE

Edmonds, J. M. *The Greek Bucolic Poets*. 1950. Reprint, Cambridge: Harvard University Press, 1970.

Gow, A. S. F. *The Greek Bucolic Poets*. Cambridge: Cambridge University Press, 1953.

Kermode, Frank, ed. *English Pastoral Poetry from the Beginnings to Marvell*. London: George G. Harrap, 1952.

Leach, Eleanor Winsor. *Vergil's Eclogues: Landscapes of Experience*. Ithaca: Cornell University Press, 1974.

Rosenmeyer, Thomas G. *The Green Cabinet: Theocritus and the European Pastoral Lyric*. Berkeley: University of California Press, 1973.

Sargent, Thelma. *The Idylls of Theocritus: A Verse Translation*. New York: W. W. Norton, 1982.

Virgil. *Eclogues. Georgics. Aenid I–VI*. Translated by H. Rushton Fairclough; revised by G. P. Goold. Cambridge: Harvard University Press, 2006.

PHILOSOPHY and PSYCHOLOGY

Bettelheim, Bruno. *The Uses of Enchantment: The Meaning and Importance of Fairy Tales*. New York: Alfred A. Knopf, 1977.

Brown, David. *God and Enchantment of Place: Reclaiming Human Experience*. New York: Oxford University Press, 2004.

Campbell, Joseph. *The Hero with a Thousand Faces*. 1949. Reprint, Novato, California: New World Library, 2008.

———. *The Masks of God: Creative Mythology*. New York: Penguin Books, 1976.

———. *The Masks of God: Occidental Mythology*. New York: Penguin Books, 1976.

———. *The Masks of God: Oriental Mythology*. New York: Penguin Books, 1976.

———. *The Masks of God: Primitive Mythology*. New York: Penguin Books, 1987.

Eibl-Eibesfeldt, Irenäus. *Love and Hate: The Natural History of Behavior Patterns*. Translated by Geoffrey Strachan. New York: Schocken Books, 1974.

Frazer, Sir James George. *The Golden Bough, A Study in Magic and Religion*. 1922. Reprint, New York: Touchstone, 1996.

Fromm, Erich. *The Forgotten Language: An Introduction to the Understanding of Dreams, Fairy Tales and Myths.* New York: Grove Weidenfeld, 1957.

Hillman, James. *Animal Presences.* Putnam, Connecticut: Spring Publications, 2008.

———. *A Blue Fire.* Edited by Thomas Moore. New York: Harper Perennial, 1991.

———. *The Thought of the Heart and the Soul of the World.* Putnam, Connecticut: Spring Publications, 2007.

Jung, C. G. *The Archetypes and the Collective Unconscious.* Translated by R. F. C. Hull. Princeton: Princeton University Press, 1990.

Kapuscinski, Ryszard. *The Other.* Translated by Antonia Lloyd-Jones. London: Verso, 2008.

Levinas, Emmanuel. *Otherwise Than Being or Beyond Essence.* Translated by Alphonso Lingis. Pittsburgh: Duquesne University Press, 2009.

Maeterlinck, Maurice. *The Treasure of the Humble.* Translated by Alfred Sutro. New York: Dodd, Mead, 1902.

Maritain, Jacques. *Creative Intuition in Art and Poetry.* 1953. New York: Meridian Books, 1955.

Midgley, Mary. *Animals and Why They Matter.* Athens: University of Georgia Press, 1983.

———. *Beast and Man: The Roots of Human Nature.* Rev. ed. London: Routledge, 2002.

———. *The Myths We Live By.* London: Routledge, 2007.

Milne, Joseph. *The Mystical Cosmos.* London: Temenos Academy, 2013.

Murdoch, Iris. *The Sovereignty of Good.* London: Routledge, 1989.

Nietzsche, Friedrich. *Thus Spoke Zarathustra.* Translated by R. J. Hollingdale. London: Penguin Books, 1969.

Panofsky, Erwin. *Meaning in the Visual Arts.* 1955. Reprint, Chicago: University of Chicago Press, 1983.

Phillips, Adam, and Barbara Taylor. *On Kindness.* New York: Farrar, Straus and Giroux, 2009.

Plato. *Euthyphro. Apology. Crito. Phaedo. Phaedrus.* Translated by Harold North Fowler. Cambridge: Harvard University Press, 1914.

Raine, Kathleen. *Defending Ancient Springs*. 1967. Reprint, West Stockbridge, Massachusetts: Lindisfarne Press, 1985.

———, and Temenos. *Lighting a Candle*. London: Temenos Academy, 2008.

Rowlands, Mark. *The Philosopher and the Wolf*. London: Granta Books, 2008.

———. *Running with the Pack*. London: Granta Books, 2013.

Theokritoff, Elizabeth. *Living in God's Creation, Orthodox Perspectives on Ecology*. Crestwood, New York: St. Vladimir's Seminary Press, 2009.

Tolstoy, Leo. *The Kingdom of God Is Within You, Christianity Not As a Mystic Religion but As a New Theory of Life*. 1894. Translated by Constance Garnett. Reprint, Lincoln: University of Nebraska Press, 1984.

SACRIFICE

Burkert, Walter. *Creation of the Sacred: Tracks of Biology in Early Religions*. Cambridge: Harvard University Press, 1998.

———. *Homo Necans: The Anthropology of Ancient Greek Sacrificial Ritual and Myth*. Translated by Peter Bing. Berkeley: University of California Press, 1983.

Daly, Robert J. *Sacrifice Unveiled: The True Meaning of Christian Sacrifice*. London: T&T Clark International, 2009.

Girard, René. *Things Hidden Since the Foundation of the World*. Translated by Stephen Bann (Books II & III) and Michael Metteer (Book I). Stanford: Stanford University Press, 1987.

———. *Violence and the Sacred*. Translated by Patrick Gregory. Baltimore: Johns Hopkins University Press, 1977.

Hubert, Henri, and Marcel Mauss. *Sacrifice: Its Nature and Function*. Translated by W. D. Halls. Chicago: University of Chicago Press, 1981.

Lienhart, Godfrey. *Divinity and Experience: The Religion of the Dinka*. Oxford: Oxford University Press, 1967.

SHEEP INDUSTRY/FUR INDUSTRY

Ewing, P. V. *Karakul Sheep, The Producers of Persian Lambskins*. Chicago: privately published, 1943.

Jones, J. Walter. *The Karakúl Sheep in America*. 1908. Ottowa: Mortimer Press, 1914.

Samet, Arthur. *Pictorial Encyclopedia of Furs: "From Animal Land to Furtown."* Rev. ed. New York: Arthur Samet, 1950.

Young, Dr. C. C. *Some Facts about Karakule Sheep.* Holliday, Texas: privately published, 1909.

ARTICLES

Friedman, Vanessa. "The Last Frontier of Chic." *Financial Times,* November 26 and 27, 2005.

Hedin, Thomas F. "Le Nostre to Mansart, Transition in the Gardens of Versailles." *Gazette des Beaux-Arts* 130 (December 1997): 191–344.

———. "The Petite Commande of 1664: Burlesque in the Gardens of Versailles." *Art Bulletin,* December 83, no. 4: 651–85.

Lush, Jay L., J. M. Jones and R. E. Diskson. "Karakul Sheep." *Texas Agricultural Experiment Station Bulletin,* no. 405 (February 1930): 1–20.

Nabours, Robert K. "The Land of Lambskins: An Expedition to Bokhara, Russian Central Asia, to Study the Karakul Sheep Industry." *National Geographic* 36, no. 1. (July 1919): 77–88.

Starr, S. Frederick. "Rediscovering Central Asia." *The Wilson Quarterly* 33, no. 3, (Summer 2009): 33–43.

Tavernise, Sabrina. "Old Farming Habits Leave Uzbekistan a Legacy of Salt." *New York Times,* June 15, 2008.